ANNA MARANDI
ARCHAEOLOGIST

DELPHI

EDITIONS
TOUBI'S®
ΕΚΔΟΣΕΙΣ

ATHENS 2000

© Copyright 2000   MICHALIS TOUBIS EDITIONS S.A.
                    Nisiza Karela, 194 00 Koropi
                    Tel. (010) 6029974, FAX: (010) 6646856
                    http://www.toubis.gr

ISBN: 960 - 540 - 350 -1

CONTENTS

DELPHI THE

The wild landscape at Delphi, with its natural grandeur
and incomparable majesty, lying at the foot of the towering Phaidriades
rocks, was the setting for the creation in ancient times of a unique
religious centre, whose fame and influence spread throughout the then
known world. This location, so richly endowed by nature, was chosen
as the site for the worship of a god whose peace-loving personality
was identified in legend with human destiny itself.
The refined aura exuded by the place cannot fail to move modern
visitors as they gaze for the first time on this unique, evocative
landscape, chosen by the ancient Greeks as the site of the omphalos
(navel) of the earth -the centre of the ancient world.
Delphi, built on the mountainside at a height of 500-570 m. above
sea level, clinging precariously to the side of Mount
Parnassos, belonged to ancient Phokis, which is today distributed between
several prefectures. The site offers a truly magnificent panoramic view.
The ancient city and its sanctuaries lie at the foot of the two enormous
Phaidriades rocks, Hyampeia at the east, now known as Phleboukos
('Flamboyant'), and Nauplia to the west, now Rodini ('Roseate').
Between the gigantic twin rocks gapes a fearsome ravine known
as Arkoudorema ('Bear stream'), from which tumbles the
crystal-clear prophetic waters of the Kastalian spring.
To the south extends the valley of the Pleistos river, and the
verdant plain of Krisa, with its countless olive-trees, which extends
from Mount Kirphys at its edge down to the sea,where the traveller's

CENTRE OF THE EARTH

eye lights upon the blue waters of the Gulf of Itea. It is no surprise that this important cross-roads was chosen by the ancient Greeks as the centre of the entire world. Modern travellers, enchanted by the grandeur of the setting, may feel that the ruins are still haunted by the shades of humble pilgrims who came to offer worship to the great god, at a sanctuary enjoying unbounded religious and spiritual influence and prestige throughout the whole of the Greek world.

Ordinary visitors cannot fail to fall under the spell of the superb back-drop chosen by the ancients for the worship of the god who inaugurated a new order and brought with him a measured moral attitude to life, sounding the innermost recesses of the human soul.

At this religious centre, the home of one of the most famous sanctuaries of ancient Greece, every aspect and manifestation of the highly anthropocentric ancient Greek civilisation was unfolded in a rare manner. Its brilliance reached as far afield as Central Asia, and the Delphic oracle, the supreme regulator of the affairs of Greece - and further afield - was deluged with lavish offerings and dedications. This was also the place chosen by Angelos Sikelianos as the headquarters for his world-wide promotion of modern Greece, stressing its ancient Greek roots and origins, inherited intact in spite of the intervening centuries.

As Sikelianos emphasised in his efforts to organise the Delphic Festivals: 'I proposed Delphi as a slogan which, thanks to its age-old origins, dynamically encloses the potential for an ideology of ecumenical influence and prestige throughout the entire world'.

The oracle and sanctuary of Delphi were built in the Archaic period in a landscape of indescribable beauty, on the sides of a ravine in a rich, highly evocative setting.

THE MYTH OF THE ORACLE

MYTHOLOGY

Zeus, the father of the gods, wished to establish the precise centre of the earth. To do so, he released two eagles from the ends of the world and the sacred birds met at Delphi, indicating the importance of the place and auguring the fame that would attend it. The site of Delphi rapidly acquired a wide reputation, mainly on account of the vapours that arose from a chasm, which induced a state of intoxication in all those who approached it. This distinctive feature of the site was the original reason for the foundation here of an oracle at which was worshipped the chthonic goddess Ge, the mother of the gods. Ge issued her prophecies through the mythical Sibyl, and later through Herophile, who was called the Pythia by Herodotus. The oracle of Ge was guarded by her son, the serpent Python. In this version of the myth, which is found mainly in Aeschylus and was the dominant version in the Classical period, Apollo is regarded as inheriting the oracle at Delphi, and not as its founder. The sanctuary was presented to Apollo as a gift by his sister, Phoebe, who had herself inherited it. Apollo's epithet Phoibos alludes to this version. The Homeric Hymn to Apollo attributes the foundation of the sanctuary to the god himself. According to this, Apollo came to the foot of the two enormous Phaidriades rocks on Parnassos after he had wandered over the whole of central Greece, and decided to found his oracle here. Before he could do so, he had to kill the serpent the Python who guarded the area. After he had killed it, legend has it that the god went into self-imposed exile for eight years, inflicting exemplary punishment on himself for the unclean act he had committed. While Apollo was absent at Tempe, his place of exile, Dionysos and his troupe came and stayed at Delphi for three months every winter and summer - the period of Apollo's punishment. According to these versions of the myth, Apollo later transformed himself into a dolphin and appeared to a group of merchants who were on a voyage from Crete. The god deliberately changed their destination and brought them to Delphi, where they served him thereafter as his attendants. Yet another version of the legend, found in Pausanias, has it that Poseidon preceded Ge and Apollo as owner of the oracle. Many gods were worshipped in the sanctuary of Apollo, and symbols such as the rock of the Sibyl, the omphalos (navel), etc. were also the object of cults.

THE MYCENAEAN PERIOD

Archaeological excavation has revealed that the site was occupied from as early as the Mycenaean period. A small, sparsely occupied village extending over the site from Kastalian Spring to the later temple of Apollo goes back to

at least the Late Helladic period (1400 BC). The archaeologist's spade has brought to light a number of chamber
tombs, potsherds, and a few small female figurines.

There is no significant
evidence in the area dating
from early prehistoric times.
There are a very few sherds
from the Neolithic period,
and all that survives
from the Early Helladic
(3000-2000 BC) and Middle
Helladic (1900-1600 BC)
periods are a few fragments
of pottery. The absence
of settlement remains,
however, is to be expected.

The centre of this Mycenaean settlement was probably in
the area of the temple of Apollo, but most of the evidence
comes from the area of the sanctuary of Athena Pronaia.
This was the site of the Mycenaean cult centre which was
presumably devoted to Apollo's predecessor at Delphi, the
first prophetess Ge, the mother goddess.

This small village was destroyed either by a rock-fall or by
fire, traces of which have been discovered in the relevant
excavation layer.

THE CONSOLIDATION OF THE DELPHIC ORACLE

The worship of Apollo became firmly rooted in the Geometric period, though the old open-air sanctuary of Ge, with
the sacred rocks, remained intact at Delphi until the end of
antiquity. The fame of the sanctuary and Apollo's oracle
began to spread throughout the whole of Greece. Beginning
in the 8th century BC, the sanctuary at Delphi quickly
reached its zenith. Its prestige and authority were accepted
by the entire the Greek world and the Delphic oracle was
inundated by lavish dedications made by pilgrims.

The Delphic oracle became powerful and important, and
developed uniquely into one of the most important factors in
Greek life, its guiding role exercising enormous influence on
political, religious, cultural, and other issues.

During the Greek colonisation period, which began in the
final decades of the 8th century BC, the Delphic oracle
played a major role as advisor.

Colonies were said to have been founded at the advice of
the Pythia in south Italy and Sicily and were founded from
places like Corinth, Sparta, and Achaea, which were near
Delphi.

After the beginning of the 7th century BC, the Delphic
oracle began to be consulted not only by would-be colonists
from the Aegean islands, and colonies were planted not only
in the west but also on the coast of Thrace and in North
Africa. At the end of the 7th century, people came to consult
the oracle from as far afield as Asia Minor. All the colonies
honoured the god Apollo with the epithet Archegetes (first
leader, founder).

The priesthood at Delphi was now recognised as the leading authority on religious questions, and all cities sought its
advice before introducing foreign cults, or instituting new
regulations for rituals. In this way the oracle facilitated the
introduction of the cult of Cybele from Phrygia and of
Hekate from Caria. It also made an important contribution

to the promotion of ethical principles and justice in the Archaic period, and the authority of the oracle was now so great that it was consulted not only by Greek kings and nobles but also by foreign rulers, who came under the influence of its fame and sent dedications or asked for prophecies. At the beginning of the 7th century BC, Midas, the legendary king of Phrygia, sent his royal throne to the sanctuary of Delphi as a gesture of respect for Apollo Pythios.

Gyges, too, the first king of the new dynasty of the Mermnadai, who ascended the throne of Sardis in 675 BC, sent many solid gold dedications to Delphi. When, according to tradition, the oracle was called upon to arbitrate between Gyges and his political rivals, it decided in favour of former, thereby showing its gratitude to his person.

The Lydian king Croesus, a descendant of Gyges, also sent rich gifts to Pythian Apollo, and Kypselos, the tyrant of Corinth, showed his devotion to the god by building the first 'treasury' at Delphi dedicated to Apollo.

The power of Delphi increased as time went on. By the end of the 7th century BC, it undoubtedly enjoyed enormous prestige and influence, and possessed great accumulated wealth. In all of this, a decisive role was played by the existence of the highly important institution of the Amphictyony.

THE DELPHIC AMPHICTYONY

Amphictyonies were associations that generally sprang from the fact that some sanctuaries also functioned as meeting places for representatives of various states.

The formation of an amphictyony was initially dictated by the need to take decisions relating to the sanctuaries, the organisation of the festivals, the building of temples, the offering of sacrifices, the management of its real estate and other matters, on which there was a suitable exchange of views. The sanctity of the site was an important factor in facilitating the convergence of views, and invocation of the deity honoured as guarantor invested the agreements reached with particular authority. In this way some amphictyonies developed into confederations of states that played an important political role. The ancient Delphic amphictyony helped to bring Greek groups together outside narrow political boundaries. Representatives met at sacred sites, initially at the sanctuary of Demeter 'Amphiktionis' near Anthele, and from the 7th century BC at the sanctuary of Apollo at Delphi (village of the Phokians).

The need to avoid subjecting the sanctuary at Delphi to any of the member-states that came together at the site led gradually to its achieving complete independence. The regular meeting of the Amphictyonic League was called the 'Pylaia' meeting, from the period when its headquarters were at Anthele, a village in the area of Thermopylai. One of the two representatives appointed by each state was called the *pylagoras*, while the second representative was known as the *hieromnemon*.

The names of the twelve participating states are given in later sources as follows: Ainianians, Achaeans, Phthiotians, Boeotians Dolopians, Dorians, Thessalians, Ionians Lokrians, Malians, Magnesians, Perrhaibians, and Phokians. At the time that they became members of amphictyony these were tribal states. Many views have been advanced on the date of the foundation of the Amphictyony. What is certain is that when the Ionians entered the Amphictyony, which at that time consisted of the Euboeans and the Athenians, they formed a Federation. This, or something of this nature, occurred before the end of 8th century BC.

The meetings of the Amphictyony took major decisions and drew up important regulations relating to the laws applying between member-states. A good example of this is the decision taken after the 8th century BC, according to which solidarity between member-states was recognised, along with the obligation on members not to destroy cities of other states belonging to the Amphictyony, even during military operations. This provision, however, was not observed.

Coin issued by the Amphictyony. Athens, Numismatic Collection of the National Archaeological Museum.

FIRST SACRED WAR

The Thessalians were the most powerful people in central Greece and aspired to control the 'gates' of Thermopylai. The Phokian city of Krisa stood in their way.

By virtue of its site, Krisa exercised control over the approach to Delphi from the sea and imposed taxes on goods in transit and pilgrims. The size, wealth and strategic position of Krisa were a threat to the independence of the small village and sanctuary. Its harbour, Kirrha, was also a lair of pirates who were the scourge of seafarers and pilgrims travelling to Delphi.

The fortifications of Krisa served as a check on the Thessalian cavalry, and this was regarded as a provocation by the Thessalians. A regular meeting of the Amphictyony decided to declare a sacred war against Krisa on the pretext of impiety. The objective was to destroy the land of Krisa, sell the inhabitants as slaves, and dedicate their territory to Leto, Artemis, and above all to Apollo and Athena Pronaia.

The main burden of the military campaigns of the First Sacred War fell upon the Thessalians on land and on the Sikyonians under Kleisthenes by sea. The war lasted for ten years and ended in 590 BC or 591 BC; according to another version, the First Sacred War was fought in the years 595-586.

The outcome of the war, of course, was that Krisa and Kirrha were destroyed and subjected to the Amphictyons, the inhabitants were sold as slaves, and the devastated land was dedicated to the Delphic gods. The territory of Krisa was proclaimed accursed and it was forbidden to till it.

The reorganisation of the Pythian Games, which were held every nine years to commemorate the killing of the serpent by Apollo and the god's flight to Tempe, is associated with the end of the First Sacred War. After the capture of Krisa, the Amphictyons assumed responsibility for the organisation of these games, and added athletic events and an equestrian contest to the existing music competition. The first Pythian Games were considered to be those held in 582 BC, when all resistance on the part of Krisa came to an end, From this time the games were be held every four years.

THE ZENITH OF THE ORACLE

In the period when the temple was reconstructed, a number of beautiful buildings were erected, one of which is the Siphnian treasury. Many brilliant buildings - dedications made by private citizens and cities, with lavish architectural relief decoration - stood in the precinct. Meanwhile, the old enclosure was extended to accommodate the new buildings, and began to assume its classical form.

Delphi in this way came to occupy a unique position in Greece and ceased to be regarded as part of the Phokian tribal group. It also retained complete control over the oracle and the priests were chosen exclusively from amongst the inhabitants of Delphi. The small town, which numbered less than 1000 inhabitants, lived by exploiting the oracle and the pilgrims. Its basic sources of revenue were the hostels, the sale of knives for sacrifices, the trade in religious goods, and the professions of stele-engraver, guide, sacrificer, and so on.

The Delphic oracle was recognised as the authentic expression of the will of the gods, not only throughout Greece, but over the whole of the then known world. Countless offerings were made by foreign rulers, though all were overshadowed by the spectacular series of dedications made by Croesus, the king of Lydia. The most brilliant of these was a lion made of pure gold, erected on a pyramid consisting of 117 slabs of 'white gold' (a mixture of gold and silver). This weighed about 250 kilos. There were also two colossal kraters, one of gold and of silver, that stood on either side of the entrance to the temple, as well as other gold and silver dedications, all of which are reported by Herodotus.

In 548 BC, the old temple in the sanctuary of Apollo was destroyed by fire. Its reconstruction was completed in 510 BC, after the intervention in 514 BC of the Alkmeonids, the great Athenian family that had been exiled by Peisistratos and his sons. The Alkmeonids completed the building at their own personal expense, using marble for the façade of the temple rather than the cheaper poros provided for in the contract.

The oracle had by now achieved its own moral stature. In the 7th century BC, the emphasis was on matters relating to murder and ritual purification. In the 6th century BC interest concentrated on the question of personal responsibility and the establishment of human limits. The authority and prestige enjoyed by the oracle throughout Greece was now beyond question.

About 505/4 BC, as part of his political reforms, Kleisthenes of Athens submitted to Delphi the names of 100 Attic heroes and the Pythia selected ten of them to be designated eponymous patrons of the new tribes.

THE DELPHIC SANCTUARY DURING THE PERSIAN WARS

During the Persian Wars Delphi and the sanctuary maintained an ambivalent stance towards the Greeks, out of a fear that they might be destroyed. Delphi medised to save itself, but attempted with some dexterity to conceal the fact. Fear of being looted induced the Delphic oracle to deliver unpleasant predictions, foretelling disaster and annihilation for the Greeks at the hands of the Persians. It nevertheless continued to play a highly important role as adviser in crucial decisions. Before the battle of Salamis in 480 BC, Themistokles managed to persuade the Athenians to evacuate Attica and rely on the Greek fleet, which was anchored off Salamis. Plutarch gives details of the role played by the oracle in this decision. According to this author, Themistokles failed to convince the Athenians at first, and then made use of divine signs to which he was able to give a suitable interpretation.

In 480 BC, during the Persian Wars, Herodotus tells us that Delphi escaped pillaging thanks to the intervention of Apollo, and attributed their salvation to a miracle: 'enormous rocks rolled down from the Phaidriades and caused the Persians to flee in panic.'

Despite the vacillating policy pursued by Delphi and its inability to offer support to the Greeks at this critical time, the moral authority of the sanctuary was unaffected, and the Greeks continued to trust the objective judgement of the god. After the victory at Salamis, the Greeks dedicated a bronze mast with three gold stars. They also dedicated a bronze statue of Apollo holding a ship's ram in his hand that was 12 cubits high.

After the end of the Persian Wars, Delphi succeeded in retaining its position as the spiritual centre of Greece. At

Herodotus relates that the Athenians sent religious ambassadors to Delphi to seek an oracle. The Pythia, Aristonike, issued a highly discouraging oracle predicting destruction for the city of Athens. The ambassadors were sunk in despair until Timon, son of Aristoboulos, advised them to enter the temple as suppliants and seek a second oracle. The Athenians followed his advice and received from the Pythia a fairly ambiguous oracle that spoke of destruction but predicted that the city would be saved in the end by a 'wooden wall'. Themistokles told the popular assembly that the phrase 'wooden wall' used by the Pythia referred to their ships, and thus succeeded in evacuating Attica and conducting the military operations at Salamis. Here the Greeks fought one of the most glorious naval engagements in history, resulting in a veritable triumph. It should be noted that Herodotus' account of the two Delphic oracles was probably composed after the event. There is a less probable view that the oracles were an invention by the ingenious Themistokles to have his plan accepted, since he considered this to be the only way of meeting the Persian threat.

this time it received a large number of honorific dedications of a highly impressive nature. One unique work of art was the dedication made by the Greeks to Pythian Apollo after the victory at Plataia. This consisted of a gold tripod placed on the top of a bronze column and depicting three intertwined snakes. On the snakes' coils were inscribed the names of the cities that fought at Plataia. It was probably on the base of the column that Pausanias carved his proud verse.

"Ἑλλήνων ἀρχηγός, ἐπεί στρατόν ὤλεσε Μήδων
Παυσανίας Φοίβῳ μνῆμ' ἀνέθηκε τόδε ὡς ἀρίστων γενομένων".

Leader of the Greeks, who destroyed the army of the Medes,
Pausanias dedicated this monument to Phoibos

According to Thucydides, this epigram by Pausanias was the main reason why he fell into disfavour, because the Spartans and other Greeks never forgave the victor of Plataia for his arrogance. Thucydides claims that the Greeks defaced the inscription and replaced it by the names of peoples. They may also have inscribed an epigram by Simonides on the base.

"Ἑλλάδος εὐρυχόρου σωτῆρες τόν δ' ἀνέθηκαν
δουλοσύνης στυγερᾶς ρυσάμενοι πόλιας".

The saviours of the spacious land of Greece
dedicated this, having rescued the cities from
loathsome slavery

The Delphic oracle experienced a period of tranquillity for the fifty years following the Persian Wars.

THE SECOND SACRED WAR

In the middle of the 5th century BC, rivalry between Athens and Sparta became acute. In 448 BC, the Spartans declared a Second Sacred War against the Phokians, since the latter had imposed their control over the sanctuary at Delphi with the aid of the Athenians. The Spartans proved victorious and handed over the sanctuary to the inhabitants of the region. After the departure of the Spartans, however, the Athenians sent a military force and restored Delphi to Phokian control.

At the beginning of the Peloponnesian War great pressure was brought to bear on Delphi to become embroiled in this dispute between Greeks. As a result, the oracle adopted a stance hostile to the Athenians.

Delphi recovered its autonomy in 421 BC. The text of the "peace of Nikias', concluded between Athens and Sparta in 421 BC and specifically intended to last for 50 years, is highly illuminating and definitive. The second clause of the treaty as reported by Thucydides prescribes

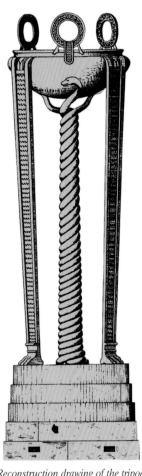

Reconstruction drawing of the tripod erected at Delphi by the Plataians.

that the temple, sanctuary and town of Delphi are to be free and autonomous.

In 373 BC the great temple of Apollo was destroyed by rocks falling from the Phaidriades as a result of a major earthquake. Responsibility for its reconstruction and economic management was assigned to a special committee called the 'temple-makers', which was appointed by the Amphictyonic Council. Work on the reconstruction of the temple began and had probably made some progress by 356 BC, when it was interrupted.

THE THIRD SACRED WAR

At any given period, the Amphictyonic Council was an apple of strife between the great powers, while the Phokians aspired to control Delphi. They asserted that Delphi was a Phokian village that ought to be returned to the Phokian League since it was the name given to a Phokian village in the Homeric 'catalogue of ships'. None of the member states of the Amphictyony, however, wanted Delphi to be annexed in this way, preferring the headquarters of the Amphictyony to be an independent, albeit small state. In 363 BC, the Amphictyony struck a blow at the party in the Delphi that wished the site to be annexed to the Phokian League.

On the proposal of the Thessalian Andronikos, it was decided to exile those citizens of Delphi who were favourable disposed towards the Phokians. This was followed by the Amphictyonic Council imposing a fine on some of the Phokians at the instigation of the Thebans. The Phokians failed to comply and during the spring of 356 BC the Council ordered the fine to be paid without further delay, and indeed threatened the Phokian state with war in the case of further failure to comply.

The decree passed by the Amphictyonic Council provoked a Phokian reaction. The most distinguished Phokian citizen, Philomelos, asserted that the fine was excessive and that the Phokians should seize Delphi themselves and make themselves masters of the oracle. Philomelos was voted 'general emperor' by the popular assembly, with unlimited authority, and chose Onomarchos as his first assistant.

With secret financial support from Sparta, Philomelos increased his mercenary army and, further aided by 1000 Phokian peltasts, seized Delphi without resistance. This action violated two Amphictyonic decisions: one condemning the provision of support to those who did not comply with decrees passed by the Amphictyony, and one forbidding the violation of the independence of Delphi.

The Lokrians of Amphissa attempted to drive out the Phokians, but without success. Philomelos then proclaimed the Amphictyonic decision relating to the Phokians to be invalid and ordered the decree to be effaced from the stele on which it had been inscribed. In June or July 356 BC he began to fortify Delphi and increased the sized of his mercenary army. In the eyes of their enemies, however, the Phokians were guilty of sacrilege; they had violated the Amphictyonic decree, had seized Delphi, and had forcibly imposed their will both on the town and in the sacred site.

The priests of Delphi practised a passive resistance by suspending funds to the oracle.

The other Amphictyons did not remain inactive in the face of these developments. In Autumn 355 BC they gathered at Thermopylai. The delegates that took part in this meeting decided unanimously to proclaim a sacred war against the Phokians. In Spring 354 BC, after some bloody conflicts, the Amphictyonic army vanquished the Phokians and Philomelos committed suicide.

In Phokis, the popular assembly elected Onomarchos 'general emperor'. Onomarchos's major source of financial support was the looting of the treasuries of the Delphic oracle. The Third Sacred War continued for ten years and gave Philip of Macedon a pretext to intervene in the affairs of southern Greece. In 346 BC Philip's intervention led to the destruction of Phokis. The town of Delphi showed its gratitude to Philip in a practical fashion. He was proclaimed 'benefactor', given the title of *proxenos* and the privilege of *promanteia* (the right to prior consultation of the oracle), and a gilded statue of him was erected. The Amphictyonic Council accorded him *proedria* (right to a front seat) at the Pythian games of 346 BC and made him a member of the Amphictyony in place of the Phokians, with the right to bequeath the privilege to his descendants.

The vicissitudes of the Delphic sanctuary were not at an end however, and peace lasted for a mere seven years.

THE FOURTH SACRED WAR
AND THE INTERVENTION OF PHILIP

After the Persian War, the Athenians had dedicated the shields that had fallen into their hands as a result of the battle, along with other booty, at the Delphic oracle. Beneath the position in which the shields were displayed they had set an inscription: 'the Athenians, from the Persians and Thebans, when they fought against the Greeks'. The Thebans had never protested about this provocative dedication. After the construction of the sanctuary of Apollo during the Third Sacred War, the Athenians restored their dedication.

At the meeting of the Amphictyonic Council of autumn 340 BC (or more probably spring 339 BC), the representatives of the western Lokrians, at the instigation of the Thebans who supported Philip, tabled a motion of censure against the Athenians, asserting that the restoration of the dedication at a time when Delphi was occupied by the Phokians, was an act of impiety. The orator Aeschines, who was *pylagoras* of the Athenian delegation, undertook to respond to the charges laid by the Lokrians. After investigation, he unearthed some very old decisions forbidding the tilling of the plain of Krisa or Kirrha. When Aeschines read out these long-forgotten decisions, the delegates were greatly disturbed, and immediately rushed to a point from which the entire plain could be seen, and were alarmed at the sight of the buildings and crops.

The following day the Amphictyons and the people of Delphi took weapons and farm implements and went to the forbidden plain, where they set about destroying all the work that had been done there. The Amphissans arrived bearing arms, however, and the Amphictyons were obliged to withdraw.

At the extraordinary meeting of June 339 BC, from which the Athenian and Boeotian representatives abstained but which was attended by the hieromnemones and *pylagores* of the other tribal groups and of Philip, the decision was taken to declare a sacred war against the Amphissans. The latter managed to delay the advance of the Amphictyonic army by promising to pay a fine and send those guilty of sacrilege into exile. The regular meeting of autumn 339 BC decided to mount another campaign against the Amphissans, to he led by Philip.

Philip was quick to seize this opportunity, his real target being the Athenians and Thebans.

These two concluded an alliance with each other out of fear of Macedonian expansionism. Philip, having first captured Amphissa and punished those guilty of impiety, moved into Central Greece and defeated the allied armies of Athens and Thebes at Chaironeia in 338 BC. Henceforth, Macedonia played a dominating role in the affairs of the oracle and of Greece in general. Philip used Delphi as a valuable. centre of political influence and on occasion consulted the oracle, but there is no indication that he attached any great importance to this activity.

Work on the reconstruction of the temple continued for some years, and it was inaugurated in 330 BC, the ceremony being attended by *theoriai* (sacred delegations) from most of the Greek cities.

THE HELLENISTIC PERIOD

The Hellenistic period of Greek history was ushered in by Alexander the Great and his successors and saw some major changes. The situation hitherto prevailing in Greece changed radically. The city-states ceased to be the dominant political units, and were dissolved or united in larger groupings, which frequently had absolutist regimes. Alongside these Hellenistic monarchies there were a number of traditional leagues or confederacies, such as the Achaean Confederacy and the Aetolian League.

Before this time, religion and mythology had been the two main sources of inspiration for the noblest creations of the Greek spirit. As time went on, however, the impetus to create new myths flagged and official religion lost its appeal and spontaneity. The trends towards critical thought and doubt were reinforced by philosophy and syncretism. These developments shook the foundations of the old beliefs. Rich gifts and offerings were still sent to Delphi, but the oracle began to lose its advisory role.

Coin struck by the Aetolian League after the victory over the Gauls in 279 BC.
It depicts the trophy erected at Delphi with the Aetolian heroine Aetolia on top.

In the 3rd century BC the Delphic sanctuary came under the domination of the Aetolian League. At this period the oracle was rarely consulted by kings or communities on great problems of state. The questions asked of it were normally connected with religious beliefs. Faith in the oracle was further undermined by the emergence of the new philosophical currents.

In 279 BC Delphi was attacked by the Gauls under Brennus, whose aim was to pillage it and seize the treasures of the oracle. The Aetolians, who repulsed the Gauls, were successors to the Macedonians and attributed the protection of the sanctuary to divine intervention. It was the god who made the barbarians take to their heels by sending flashes of lightning and causing rock falls. To commemorate the great victory, the Aetolians, the new masters of the sanctuary, established a new festival called the Soteria, which was celebrated every four years in honour of Zeus Soter and Apollo.

The kings of Pergamon showed particularly great respect for Delphi, and made many dedications in the sanctuary. They also enriched it with offerings and stoas, took an interest in the arts and letters, and of course erected statues of themselves at conspicuous positions inside the Delphic sanctuary.

DELPHI IN THE ROMAN PERIOD

In 191 BC the Aetolians were expelled by the Romans, who assumed control of the oracle. This marked the beginning of a new period for Delphi and for the whole of

Greece. In 168 BC the Roman general Aemilius Paulus defeated Perseus, the last king of Macedonia, at Pydna and established Rome as the arbitrator of Greek affairs. At Delphi, Aemilius Paulus erected an equestrian statue of himself on the high pedestal prepared by Perseus to receive his own statue.

During the Roman period, many of the Greek cities at which there were large sanctuaries, such as Delphi and Athens, which was a Roman ally, continued to be autonomous city-states.

The Romans, however, bore a large part of the responsibility for the decline into which the great Greek sanctuaries entered in the 1st century BC. They proved incapable of preventing the sacking of Delphi both by barbarians and by the Roman emperors themselves.

An attack on Delphi by the Gauls in 109 BC was repulsed by Minucius Rufus. In 87/86 BC, when Sulla was besieging Athens, in order to cover his expenses incurred during the Mithridatic wars, he seized large sums from the treasuries of Delphi, including a silver pithos dedicated by Croesus. This was officially a loan, but the Greeks soon learned that the Roman generals would no longer protected their sanctuaries but were concerned to strip them bare.

Delphi was attacked in 83 BC by a Thracian tribe, the Maidoi, who sacked the town and torched the temple. According to tradition this was the first time that the 'undying fire', which had burned for centuries in the temple, went out, and the temple itself suffered significant damage.

The town could not avoid its inevitable decline. The Roman emperors were faced with a very complex situation at Delphi. Augustus and the other emperors who sought to secure the continuation of Greek traditions found themselves obliged to revive a sacred oracle, a town and a federation.

Alongside his attempts to restore the cults, Augustus also restored the Amphictyony. In the 1st century AD (AD 67), Nero visited Delphi as part of his notorious tour of the Greek games, and took part in the Pythian games. The authorities of the Delphic sanctuary had no scruples in equating Nero with Herakles, and for his visit had relief depictions of the symbolic labours of the god carved on marble slabs in the orchestra of the theatre. Despite this, Nero ordered the looting of the treasures adorning the sanctuary. He had 500 bronze statues removed from the temple and taken to Rome to adorn his new palace, the 'Golden House'. He also established a colony of Roman veterans at the city.

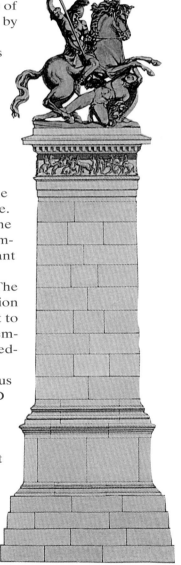

Reconstruction drawing
of the column of Aemilius Paulus.

23

Plutarch, who served as priest of Apollo at Delphi in the late 1st and early 2nd century AD, tells us that whereas at its height the sanctuary needed two or three priestesses to issue oracles, in his day one Pythia was enough.

The Roman authorities took some important steps to maintain the sanctuary. In AD 90, Domitian repaired the temple and significant measures were taken later to preserve the reputation of the Pythian games, and indeed of all the events that redounded to the glory of Delphi. This was especially true under Hadrian, Septimius Severus, and Caracalla.

In AD 125, Hadrian decreed that the Pythian games should continue to be held. Along with the Isthmian, Nemean and, of course, the Olympic games, these were the most important of the traditional games in Greece.

The Pythian games endured and their fame was undiminished - evidence for the preservation of the cultural unity, albeit superficial, of a weary Greece, supported by the Roman emperors.

Under Hadrian, the Greek East experienced a new period of longer-lasting prosperity and well-being. Hadrian was a philhellene who engaged in extensive building activity in Greece. At his orders, important structures were erected in the new district of Pylaia at Delphi, during his visits to the city.

The emperor was particularly attentive to the organisation and maintenance of the city, the exploitation of its water sources, and above all for the reforestation of its land and the terms on which property could be bequeathed.

Herodes Atticus and the Antonine emperors also contributed to a regeneration of the city and the sanctuary through their generosity.

Nevertheless, there was a reduction in the business conducted by the oracle during the Roman period. The main causes of this were a tendency to scepticism and the competition it suffered from private fortune-tellers.

Generally speaking, Delphi enjoyed close relations with Rome, based to a large degree on mutual respect. From the very first, the emperors had understood that the moral authority of the ancient sanctuary would serve as an ideal support for their policies, and this determined the level of their relations.

Naturally, relations between Delphi and the Romans were not always good. Nero's behaviour in particular dispelled any false impressions the inhabitants may have entertained that they would receive privileged treatment. In Roman times, Delphi placed great importance on visits by the so-called men of letters of the day, the orators, poets, and sophists, and took pride in the statues dedicated to them. The city continued to aspire to be the centre and repository of Hellenism, a respected meeting-point, a valued receiver of the cultural tradition.

Between AD 342 and 344, Flavius Felicianus, the priest of Apollo, received assurances from the Praetorian guard that the sanctuary would be protected against Christian rioters. These assurances reflected Rome's desire to associate itself with one of the most glorious and famous sanctuaries of the ancient world.

THE INEVITABLE END
OF THE DELPHIC SANCTUARY

The Delphic sanctuary was moving towards its inevitable end. Although Constantine the Great was honoured at Delphi, he removed countless works of art from the sanctuary to adorn his new capital, Constantinople. And when the emperor Julian sent his friend, the doctor Oreibasios, to Delphi to seek an oracle from the Pythia, the decline was by now irreversible.

Tell the king that the elegant building has fallen,
Phoibos no longer has a home, nor a laurel of prophecy,
nor a speaking spring; the speaking water has been extinguished.

Despite the concern showed by the Romans, Delphi could not escape decline. Constantine established Christianity as the official religion of the empire, and there was no place in the new religion for Apollo. The traditional institutions and the new institutions introduced by the Romans fell into disuse.

In the 4th century AD the priest at Delphi sought protection from the Roman authorities, in an attempt to preserve freedom of religion. But the new world had adopted Christianity and had come down firmly on the side of the new religion.

The spirit of Delphi was dead. Theodosius the Great issued an edict in AD 394 closing all the sanctuaries and condemning ancient religion. After this the area was covered with earth deposits caused by landslides.

As time went by, the works of art and buildings at Delphi were plundered and destroyed. For some time Delphi was occupied by a Christian community, and was finally abandoned completely in the 7th century AD.

A village called Kastri was created on the site of the ancient sanctuary. It was not until 15 centuries later that the archaeologist's spade brought to light the ruins of the most venerable sanctuary of ancient Greece, the mirror of Hellenism, the sanctuary that stood at the centre of the world.

THE ORACLE

THE
ORACLE

CLEROMANCY

THE
PYTHIAN GAMES

THE ORACLE

The Delphic oracle was beyond question the most famous oracular centre in the ancient world and retained its prestige and influence until the end of antiquity.

An indication of the reputation and fame enjoyed by Delphi is provided by the fact that every known form of prophecy was attributed to it by the ancient authors.

According to tradition, Parnassos, the hero who gave his name to the mountain at Delphi, was the first to discover the art of prophesying from the flight of birds. Delphos and Amphiktyon, who gave their names to the city and the Amphictyonic League, discovered how to prophesy by examining entrails and interpreting dreams and omens. The Pyrkooi, who were local priests, also read auguries in the flames of sacrifices. The Thriai, too, winged maidens who prophesied by eating honey, were associated by Philochoros with the prophetic pebbles *(thriai)* used at Delphi for the practice of cleromancy, or divination by lot.

Inspired ecstatic prophecy was a typical feature of the cult of Apollo, and in early times was exercised in other places through the medium of a man. The choice of a woman to fulfil this role at Delphi is to be interpreted in the light of the pre-existing cult of the goddess Ge in the region, which was ultimately accepted by the priesthood at Delphi.

The fame of the oracle in the Classical period was based on the Pythia. In the ancient literary sources, the Pythia is rarely presented as an individual personality, because she was not supposed to utter the oracles consciously: her personality was temporarily displaced by Apollo, and she simply spoke at the god's inspiration and in his name. She was, that is, simply the god's medium of expression.

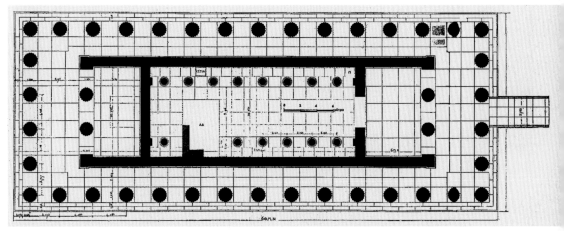

Plan of the Temple of Apollo.

*Reconstruction drawing
of the east facade
of the Temple of Apollo.*

The earliest literary reference to the Pythia is by the poet Theognis. Diodorus Siculus tells us that the Pythia was originally a young maiden. On one occasion, however, Echekrates of Thessaly fell in love with her, abducted her, and raped her. After this the people of Delphi passed a law that no virgin was to assume the duties of the Pythia. She was henceforth to be a woman of over fifty years of age, but was to dress in white, as a virgin, in memory of the earlier young prophetess.

From the time she assumed her duties the Pythia had to lead a blameless life. After her election, she had to leave her husband and children and obey a series of confining regulations. She had to live in her own house inside the sanctuary, observe religious rules, and lead a life devoted entirely to the god and her sacred duties.

Plutarch states that there was no set method for selecting the Pythia, and the priestess was not drawn from some particular aristocratic or other family. She was an ordinary villager, who need not have any special gifts or education.

Originally there was only one Pythia, but later, when the oracle was at the height of its fame and the numbers of pilgrims increased, there were three to meet the demand.

One of the most common honours accorded by the city of Delphi to states or individuals was the right of *promanteia*, or priority in consulting the oracle.

Delphi naturally had the right of first consultation, but the city frequently awarded the second place to a favoured city or person. This right of priority of consultation was considered a very great honour.

There was a fixed procedure for the seeking and issuing of an oracle, which bound both the Pythia and the *theopropos*, the word used to designate the person seeking the prophecy.

According to Plutarch's description, procedure lasted all day, from dawn to dusk. At dawn, the Pythia prepared for the consultation by purifying herself by bathing in the Kastalian spring. The prophetai and hosioi (priests) who would attend the issuing of the oracle, also bathed themselves in the Kastalian spring. Next, the Pythia immersed herself in the smoke of laurel leaves and barley-flour burning on the sacred hearth. According to tradition, the Pythia drew her inspiration from chewing on laurel leaves or by drinking sacred water.

As another aspect of the preliminary ritual, the priests established whether the god Apollo was favourably inclined to receive a request for an oracle.

Themis and Aigaia. In this reconstruction, Themis holds a bowl in her hands, containing water from the sacred spring, and a branch of the holy laurel. These are the symbols of the Pythia's prophetic powers. (5th c. BC. Berlin Archaeological Museum).

The method used for this was to make an offering of a goat. Before it was sacrificed, the animal had to give a good omen by quivering from head to foot. To achieve this end, it was sprinkled with cold water, the process being repeated until the desired omen was attained, or until it became clear that it was not a favourable day on which to seek an oracle. The purpose of the ritual was obviously to get the animal to shudder in the same way as the Pythia shuddered in her ecstasy. The animal had to be sound in limb and have no natural defects; if these conditions were met and the animal did in the end shiver violently, this was an infallible sign that it was an auspicious day for an oracle. If this did not happen, all questions were cancelled for that day.

When the required omen had been achieved, the beast was sacrificed outside the temple, probably on the altar dedicated by the Chians, so that everyone would know that the day was a favourable one. The Pythia was then given permission to enter the temple, drank water from the Kastalian or Kassotis spring, chewed laurel leaves, and then climbed up on to the tripod.

The tripod is generally given particular prominence. It was used by Apollo, especially at Delphi, as a throne. Art and literature present the god sitting in the bowl, and this was precisely the position adopted by the Pythia when she was prophesying. Why the god turned the tripod into his seat is not easy to divine. What is certain is that the Pythia sat on the tripod while prophesying because at that point she had no existence of her own but was serving as the god's instrument, through whom he expressed his will.

Meanwhile, the officials of the Delphic oracle also purified themselves in the Kastalian spring. According to the ancient sources, the body of officiating priests consisted of a high-priest, who was called prophetes, the priests, or *hosioi*, and a number of representatives of Delphi, chosen by lot.

Finally, all the pilgrims who had come to seek an oracle bathed themselves in the same spring, because they were not allowed to consult the oracle until they had done so. The order of consultation sometimes depended on rights of *promanteia*, and was sometimes established by drawing lots.

Once everyone was ready, a festive procession was formed and headed for the temple. For the faithful to be admitted to the temple, they had to offer a kind of consecrated bread on the altar called *pelanos*, which was sold at a high price. This was the minimum they had to pay in order to consult the oracle. After this, the pilgrim was ushered into the interior of the temple accompanied by the *pro-*

ATHENS 2004

OFFICIAL LICENSED OLYMPIC KEEPSAKES ATHENS 2004

- **POSTERS**
- **CARDS**
- **CALENDARS**
- **COLLECTIONS IN FOLDERS**

Central distribution: Sina & Skoufa 67, P.C.: 106 80 Kolonaki, Tel./Fax: 210 36 06186. Also available in selected stores.

http://www.toubis.gr

xenos, the priests, and the representative of his own city, who would offer him advice during the ritual. Here on the altar on which burned the undying fire, he had to offer a sacrifice as a token of his faith in and respect for the god.

In prehistoric times, the residents of Delphi kept part of the sacrificial victim for themselves.

After the offer of the sacrifice, the questioner was led ceremonially into the adyton of the temple, at the back of the cella. Here the Pythia sat on the sacred tripod, the god's throne, which was placed over the mouth of the chasm. No woman was allowed to enter the adyton. The questioner sat in the nearest corner of the room and had to follow the advice he had been given and 'think pure thoughts and speak words of good omen'. The Pythia could be seen neither by the pilgrim nor by the *prophetes*, for she was concealed behind a screen and was already in an unaccustomed, mysterious state of ecstasy.

The *prophetes* submitted the question - which he had already received it in either written or oral form - to the Pythia, and transmitted her response to the questioner. It is not clear from the sources whether the latter could hear clearly what the Pythia said. Some references reveal that she did not speak in a normal voice but shouted and cried aloud, giving her response in inarticulate, incomprehensible, disconnected words, having already fallen into a trance. Her own personality had been displaced for the time and her own individuality had become a vehicle for the god to reveal his unerring will. The *prophetes* interpreted her utterances and traditionally expressed them in hexameter verses. When the response had been given, the pilgrim left the temple. The Pythia's answers were obscure and ambiguous, and believers could interpret them as they wished. The ora-

Reconstruction drawing of the adyton.

cle's abstruse replies have become legendary, and it needed prophetic powers to interpret them. Only the passage of time would confirm, or give the lie to the interpretations offered. This accounts for the epithet Loxias (crooked) given to Apollo.

The authorities of Delphi never gave any official explanation or clarification, and the person who had consulted the oracle had to have recourse to interpreters in his own country or elsewhere to have the oracle explained to him.

It was widely accepted that the god spoke in riddles. Most of the oracular responses that have been preserved are expressed in the first person, because the Pythia was not answering consciously but was simply a medium for the words of the god.

A good example of an obscure, ambiguous response is the one given to Croesus, when he was waging war with Cyrus, which is preserved by Herodotus: 'If Croesus crosses the (river) Halys, he will destroy a mighty empire.' Croesus interpreted the oracle favourably to himself and declared war on the Persians, but the empire he destroyed was not that of Cyrus, as he had believed, but his own, the kingdom of Lydia.

Depiction of Croesus from an amphora dating from c. 500 BC. Paris, Louvre Museum.

The view that the Pythia prophesied in an ecstatic or hypnotic trance has been disputed, since neither the water of the spring nor laurel leaves induce this condition; nor has the sacred chasm from which, according to tradition, fumes issued and put the Pythia in a trance, been identified in the adyton of the temple. It has accordingly been asserted that after drinking the water and chewing the laurel leaves, the Pythia merely came under the influence of Apollo, who spoke through her mouth.

Plutarch tells us that in very early times the Pythia gave responses on only one day a year, the seventh day of the Delphic month Bysios (February-March), which coincided with the beginning of spring. The day itself was regarded as Apollo's birthday.

From the 6th century onwards, however, the increased demand on the oracle lead to responses being given on the 7th day of every month, apart from the three winter months, when Apollo left Delphi and went to the Hyperboreans. During these months, the god gave the sanctuary to Dionysos, the god of festivities and drinking.

CLEROMANCY

As we have seen, genuine ecstatic prophesy is attested at Delphi in historical times. The method practised earlier was cleromancy, which made use of sacred lots (*kleroi*) or pebbles (*thriai*). This method also continued in use in historical times, when the numbers of those seeking the advice of the god were so great that they could not be satisfied in the brief period of nine days available each year.

Generally speaking, cleromancy had a very long association with Delphi. The Thriai, the Nymphs who personified the lots, are said to have dwelt on Parnassos and raised Apollo. This kind of prophesying was devised by Apollo himself when he was still a child. Before they made their prophesy, the Thriai used to eat honey, which was believed to produce an ecstatic trance. (Pindar uses the word 'bees' of the priestesses of Apollo in the sanctuary at Delphi.)

The prophetic pebbles were kept in the bowl of the sacred tripod. One pebble was either drawn from the bowl on the tripod or was caused to fall out of it by moving the bowl.

The oracle issued was always based on the interpretation of the signs on the pebble that had been drawn from the bowl.

Cleromancy was practised on the other days of the month, when the Pythia was not sitting on the tripod to issue her oracle. The lots drawn were probably beans painted white or black, representing favourable or unfavourable responses respectively. Alternatively they might have the names written on them of rulers, heroes, or gods to whom the interested party should offer sacrifice.

The fact that there are very few references to this method of divination in the written sources suggests that cleromancy was less widely known and less important than ecstatic prophesy. The ritual of cleromancy was possibly practised in public and may have been carried out by the Pythia in the open court of the temple, or in the stoa at the entrance. The ecstatic prophesies issued by the Pythia, which were given on only one day each month, were obviously surrounded by great brilliance and a carefully organised ceremony. Cleromancy, on the other hand, took place on most days for nine months of the year, was less costly and wearisome, and could not be declared unsuccessful or ill-omened.

When reference is made to Delphic oracles, this clearly implies only words issued by the great god through the medium of his inspired prophetess seated upon the tripod, his sacred throne.

THE PYTHIAN GAMES

The Delphic sanctuary was the home of the second most important of the pan-Hellenic games, the Pythian games. The beginnings of these games are lost amidst various versions of the myth. Their purpose was to commemorate the god's victory over the Python, and his flight to seek purification in the vale of Tempe.

The Pythian games were originally held every eight years and consisted exclusively of music competitions, involving hymns in honour Apollo accompanied by the lyre. After the First Sacred War, the games were reorganised by the Amphictyonic League along the lines of the Olympic games and were now held every four years. Equestrian and athletic contests also began to be held alongside the musical contests.

The prize for the victors in the Pythian Games was a wreath of laurel, Apollo's tree, taken from branches cut from the oldest laurel at Tempe by a boy both of whose parents were still alive. The games were held in the third year of the Olympic cycle, in the second Delphic month, Boukatios (August-September) and from the fourth century BC onwards in the fourth Delphic month of Heraios (October). Before they began, a sacred truce lasting three months was proclaimed between all Greeks, involving a cease-fire in any military hostilities, in order to honour the great god. Every city sent a sacred delegation called a *theoria*. Quite independently of the Pythian Games, the Athenians sent a special *theoria* called the Pythais to Delphi, and organised separate festivals and theatrical performances.

The Pythian games lasted from six to eight days, and Plutarch tells us that the first day was given over to the Septerion. It opened with the sacrificing of three bulls, which was followed by re-enactment of the killing of the Python by Apollo. On the second day 100 bulls were sacrificed in honour of Apollo. A great procession was formed of priests and the representatives of the cities, athletes, and the entire crowd of pilgrims, which moved ritually to the great temple of Apollo where the hecatomb was offered on the great altar dedicated by the Chians. The third day was given over to a ritual banquet at which everyone eat the meat of the victims sacrificed the previous day. On the fourth day were held the music competition and performances of plays, the former involving hymns in honour of the god accompanied by a lyre or flute. The fifth and sixth days were devoted to the athletic contests, that is, the *stadion* (a sprint of about 200 m.), *diaulos* (twice the *stadion*), *dolichos* (long-distance race), pentathlon, wrestling, boxing and Pankration, while the seventh day was reserved for the equestrian contests, the most brilliant of all the events. These might run into an eighth day if they could not be completed on time. The names of the victors of the Pythian Games were inscribed on tablets and they won the right to erect a statue of themselves within the sanctuary. The most important of the musical contests involved playing the kithara, an instrument associated closely with Apollo, and the event known as the Pythia melody, a re-enactment of the killing of the Pytho. The athletic and equestrian contests were originally held in plain of Krisa.

In the second half of the 5th century BC, however, the stadium was built at the foot of the Phaidriades rocks, and the athletic and possibly also the music contests began to be held in this. Later still, the music contests were held in the theatre. The first Pythian Games were held in the 582 BC, when the winner of the chariot race was Kleisthenes the tyrant of Sikyon, who dedicated his chariot to the great god after his victory.

Flautist and bard in a flute-playing contest. Black-figure pelike of the 6th c. BC. New York, Metropolitan Museum.

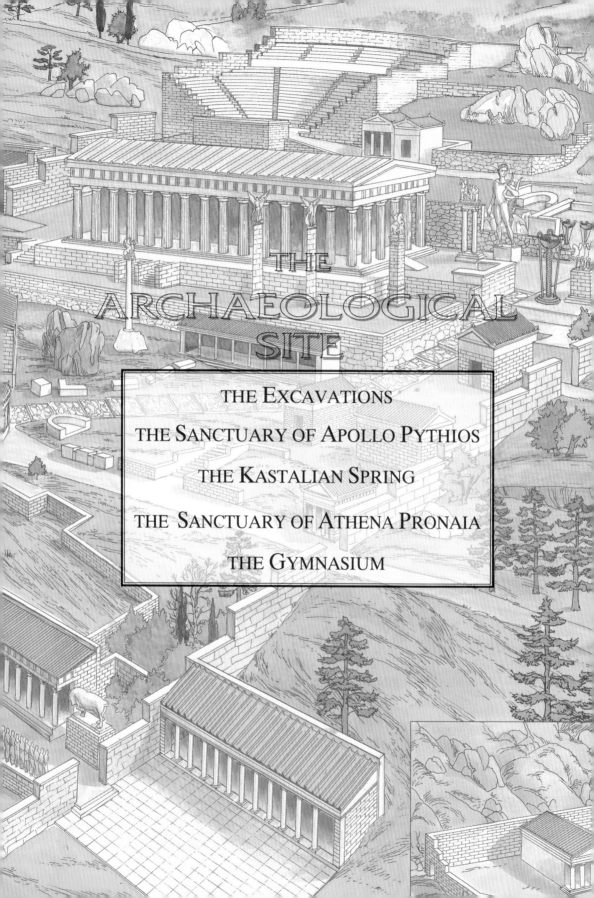

THE
ARCHAEOLOGICAL
SITE

THE EXCAVATIONS

The ruins of the famous sanctuary at Delphi have been brought to light by excavations conducted by the French Archaeological School. Before this several foreign travellers and archaeologists of all nationalities had visited Delphi, beginning in the 15th century AD. The first investigation of the ruins was begun in 1840, by the Germans O. Muller and E. Curtius. This rather limited-scale work was continued by the Frenchmen Wescher and Foucart in 1860, and Haussoulier in 1880, and the German Pomtow in 1887. These scholars brought important evidence to light and wrote important, substantial studies.

Serious archaeological excavation, however, required removing the small village of Kastri which was built above the ruins. A major factor in achieving this precondition was the devastating earthquake of 1870, as a result of which the inhabitants of the village asked to be moved elsewhere. It was at this time that the Greek Archaeological Service showed its first interest in the investigation of the site and the first efforts were made to move the village to a different location.

In 1891, a permit to excavate Delphi was granted to the French Archaeological School, which was vying with the Americans and Germans, who were also interested. The excavations were directed by Th. Homolle.

Systematic work began in 1892 after the expropriation of the small village by the Greek government and its removal to its present site. The meticulous, painstaking excavations revealed the sanctuary of Apollo with all the significant monuments that had escaped destruction and provide us with revealing valuable evidence for the past. The results of the excavation were published by the French Archaeological School of Athens.

Photographs from the first excavation efforts at Delphi site.

The outstanding archaeological site at Delphi has a wealth of ancient monuments and is of unique beauty. It forms an open-air museum that in a wide variety of ways encapsulates the whole of ancient Greek art and history.

PLAN OF THE ARCHAEOLOGICAL
SITE OF DELPHI

1. Bull of the Corcyreans.
2. Dedication of the Arkadians.
3. Monument of the Spartans.
4. Trojan Horse.
5. Dedication of the Athenians.
6. The Seven against Thebes.
7. The Epigonoi.
8. The Kings of Argos.
9. Hellenistic monument.
10. Bronze statue of Philopoimen.
11.-12. Two statue bases.
13.-14. Two recesses.
15. Monument of the Tarentines.
16. Treasury of the Sikyonians.
17. Building complex of the Knidians.
18. Dedication of the Aetolians.
19. Treasury of the Siphnians.
20. Dedication of the Liparaians.
21. Treasury of the Thebans.
22. Rectangular recess.
23. Treasury of the Boeotians.
24. Treasury of the Megarians.
25. Treasury of the Syracusans.
26. Treasury of the Klazomenians.
27. Treasury of the Knidians.
28α. Stone omphalos.
28. Treasury of the Potidaians.
29. Unidentified Archaic treasury.
30. Treasury of the Athenians.
31. Asklepieion.
32. Ancient fountain.
33. Bouleuterion.
34. Exedra of Herodes Atticus.
35. Spring in the sanctuary of Ge.
36. Rock of the Sibyl.
37. Dedication of the Boeotians.
38. Exedras.
39. Monument with three columns.
40. Unidentified Archaic treasury.
41. Sphinx of the Naxians.
42. Stoa of the Athenians.
43. Treasury of the Corinthians.
44. Treasury of the Cyrenaians.
45. Prytaneion.
46. Unidentified Archaic treasury.
47. Treasury of Brasidas and the Akanthians.
48. Monument of the Tarentines (second).
49. Tripod of the Plataians.
50. Chariot of the Rhodians.
51. Unidentified Archaic treasury.
52. Dedication of the Messenians of Naupaktos.
53. Monument of Aemilius Paulus.
54. Stoa of Attalos I.
55. 'Oecus of Attalos' (Dionysion).
56. Dedication of Attalos I.
57. Statue of Attalos I.
58. Statue of Eumenes II.
59. Unidentified treasury.
60. Altar of the Chians.
61. Bronze Palm-tree.
62. Monument of Aristaineta.
63. Base of the statue of Prusias.
64. Apollo Sitalias.
65. Tripods of the Deinomenids.
66. Kassotis (spring).
67. Statues of Aetolian generals.
68. Base of the Corcyreans.
69. Horseshoe-shaped base.
70. Dedication of Daochos II.
71. Archaic polygonal wall.
72. Column with dancing girls.
73. Base of an unknown dedication.
74. Precinct of Neoptolemos.
75. Stone of Kronos.
76. Monument of the 4th c. BC.
77. Lesche of the Knidians.
78. Remains of a dedication of the Messenians.
79. Temple of Apollo.
80. Sanctuary of the Muses.
81.-85. Unidentified Archaic treasuries.
88. Dedication of Krateros.
89-90. Large stoa of the Athenians.
91. Unidentified treasury.
92. Theatre.
93-94. Unidentified treasuries.
95. Potidanion.

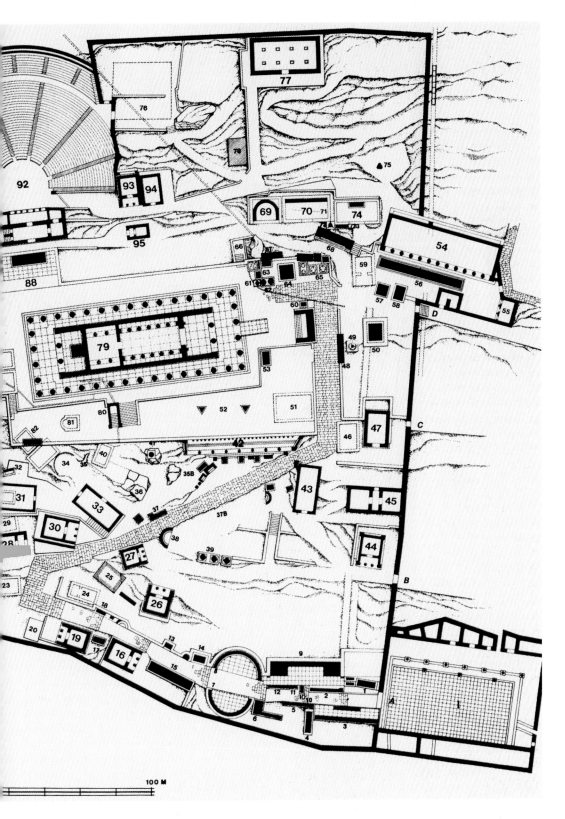

100 M

Reconstruction of the archaeological site at Delphi.

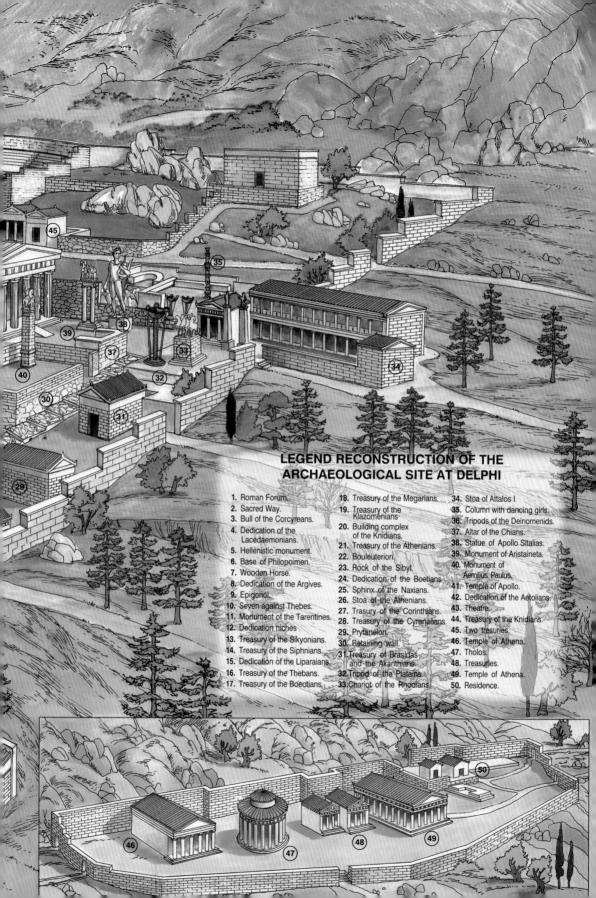

LEGEND RECONSTRUCTION OF THE ARCHAEOLOGICAL SITE AT DELPHI

1. Roman Forum.
2. Sacred Way.
3. Bull of the Corcyreans.
4. Dedication of the Lacedaemonians.
5. Hellenistic monument.
6. Base of Philopoimen.
7. Wooden Horse.
8. Dedication of the Argives.
9. Epigonoi.
10. Seven against Thebes.
11. Monument of the Tarentines.
12. Dedication niches
13. Treasury of the Sikyonians.
14. Treasury of the Siphnians.
15. Dedication of the Liparaians.
16. Treasury of the Thebans.
17. Treasury of the Boeotians.

18. Treasury of the Megarians.
19. Treasury of the Klazomenians
20. Building complex of the Knidians.
21. Treasury of the Athenians.
22. Bouleuterion.
23. Rock of the Sibyl.
24. Dedication of the Boetians.
25. Sphinx of the Naxians.
26. Stoa of the Athenians.
27. Trasury of the Corinthians.
28. Treasury of the Cyrenaeans.
29. Prytaneion
30. Retaining wall.
31. Treasury of Brasidas and the Akanthians.
32. Tripod of the Plataians.
33. Chariot of the Rhodians.

34. Stoa of Attalos I.
35. Column with dancing girls.
36. Tripods of the Deinomenids.
37. Altar of the Chians.
38. Statue of Apollo Sitalias.
39. Monument of Aristaineta.
40. Monument of Aemilius Paulus.
41. Temple of Apollo.
42. Dedication of the Aetolians.
43. Theatre.
44. Treasury of the Knidians.
45. Two tresuries.
46. Temple of Athena.
47. Tholos.
48. Treasuries.
49. Temple of Athena.
50. Residence.

THE SANCTUARY OF APOLLO PYTHIOS

The sanctuary of Apollo, the revered precinct of the great god, lies at the foot of Rodini, one of the Phaidriades, beneath the awe-inspiring towering rock. The Delphic sanctuary was enclosed within a built wall, in which there were many gates. The masonry was in places the polygonal of the 6th century BC, and in others, on the south side for example, the pseudo-isodomic of the 5th century BC. The enclosure, which was situated on rising ground, was quadrilateral, or rather trapezoidal, in form. The irregular south side was the shortest, and its greatest dimensions are 195 x 135 m.

The 'sacred precinct of Apollo' did not received any remodelling over the years, except for the extensions required to house the dedications of Attalos I on the east side and stoa of the Aetolians on the west side in the 3rd century BC. A Sacred Way winds through the entire sanctuary. The main entrance is at the south-east corner (between the Museum and the Kastalia spring). Modern visitors use the same entrance as the one through which pilgrims passed in ancient times.

In front of the main entrance is a rectangular paved square of late Roman date. On the north side of this were Ionic stoas with shops at the back, parts of which are still preserved today. In this **Roman forum** were probably sold objects relating to the cult of Apollo, such as small figurines, tripods, etc., which were purchased by pilgrims who wished to offer them to the god.

In later times, majestic processions formed here for the various festivals held in the sanctuary, such as the Pythian games. Architectural members, statue bases, and some of the Ionic columns from the north stoa, which was restored in 1977, are all that now survive of the grandeur of former days.

The Sacred Way that leads up to the sanctuary of Apollo begins at the main gate of the sanctuary, in front of which there are four steps. It is 4-5 m. wide, and is at a lower level today than it was originally; the pavement goes back to the Byzantine period, by which time the Delphic sanctuary was in decline. On either side of the Sacred Way stood the treasuries and votive monuments erected by various ancient Greek cities. These were at once a token of their respect for and belief in the great god, and of the financial prosperity of the cities who dedicated them.

The Roman forum.

The Sacred Way.

They are all minor masterpieces, many of them set in particularly privileged conspicuous positions, though others had less well-favoured sites; all of them symbolised the power and prosperity of the cities that dedicated them.

The first monument to the right after the main entrance is the remains of the stone pedestal of the **Bull of Corcyra.** The bronze bull that stood on the pedestal was the work of the Aeginetan sculptor Theopropos, and was dedicated by the Corcyreans about 580 BC. Pausanias states that the work was dedicated as a tithe from the profits of a large haul of fish (tunny), because a bull had been the occasion of this catch of many tons of fish.

The pedestal measures 4 x 5.20 m., is preserved to a lesser height than it would have been originally, and, as we learn from the inscription on its north side, has stood here since the 4th century BC.

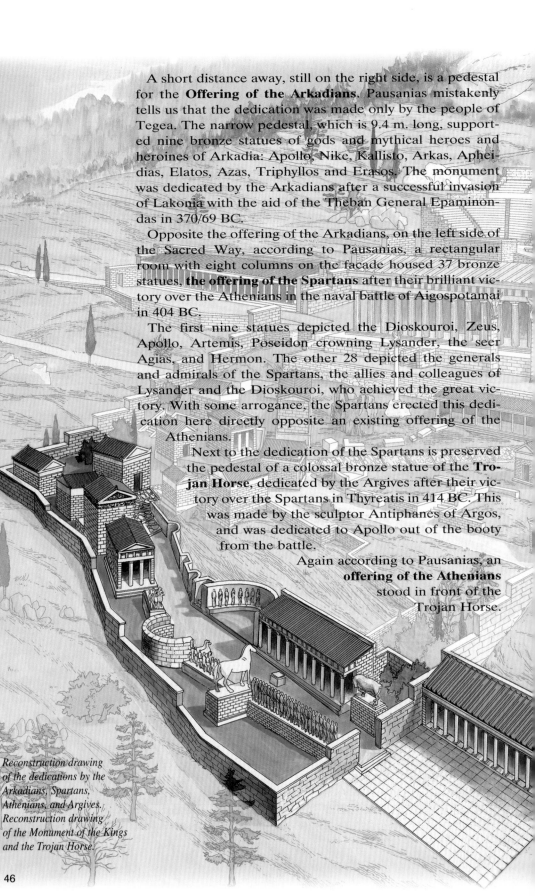

A short distance away, still on the right side, is a pedestal for the **Offering of the Arkadians**. Pausanias mistakenly tells us that the dedication was made only by the people of Tegea. The narrow pedestal, which is 9.4 m. long, supported nine bronze statues of gods and mythical heroes and heroines of Arkadia: Apollo, Nike, Kallisto, Arkas, Apheidias, Elatos, Azas, Triphyllos and Erasos. The monument was dedicated by the Arkadians after a successful invasion of Lakonia with the aid of the Theban General Epaminondas in 370/69 BC.

Opposite the offering of the Arkadians, on the left side of the Sacred Way, according to Pausanias, a rectangular room with eight columns on the facade housed 37 bronze statues, **the offering of the Spartans** after their brilliant victory over the Athenians in the naval battle of Aigospotamai in 404 BC.

The first nine statues depicted the Dioskouroi, Zeus, Apollo, Artemis, Poseidon crowning Lysander, the seer Agias, and Hermon. The other 28 depicted the generals and admirals of the Spartans, the allies and colleagues of Lysander and the Dioskouroi, who achieved the great victory. With some arrogance, the Spartans erected this dedication here directly opposite an existing offering of the Athenians.

Next to the dedication of the Spartans is preserved the pedestal of a colossal bronze statue of the **Trojan Horse**, dedicated by the Argives after their victory over the Spartans in Thyreatis in 414 BC. This was made by the sculptor Antiphanes of Argos, and was dedicated to Apollo out of the booty from the battle.

Again according to Pausanias, an **offering of the Athenians** stood in front of the Trojan Horse.

Reconstruction drawing of the dedications by the Arkadians, Spartans, Athenians, and Argives. Reconstruction drawing of the Monument of the Kings and the Trojan Horse.

This commemorated the victory at the Battle of Marathon and honoured the Athenian general Miltiades. It included 16 statues, depicting Athena, Apollo, the victor Miltiades, and the seven eponymous heroes of Athens. These statues, the work of Pheidias, were not erected immediately after the victory at Marathon. The offering was made several years later from a tithe of the booty won at the battle at Marathon, possibly at the time of Kimon in about 460 BC, when Militades' reputation had been restored.

The statues of three new eponymous heroes – King Antigonos of Macedonia, Demetrios Poliorketes, and King Ptolemy of Egypt - were added much later.

Two more **offerings of the Argives** were erected next to the Trojan Horse. The first included seven statues set on a straight base, depicting the Seven against Thebes - the legendary Argive leaders of the Argives in the campaign against Thebes which overthrew Eteokles - and was dedicated after the Argive victory over Sparta at Oinoe in 456 BC. One of the statues depicted Amphiaraos in his chariot, led by the charioteer Baton. They were all financed from the spoils of the battle of Oinoe, and were the work of the sculptors Hypatodoros and Aristogeiton.

The second offering of the Argives, which stood next to it according to Pausanias, was also financed by the spoils seized from the Spartans after the battle of Oinoe (456 BC). This is a group of statues set on a semicircular base 12 m. in diameter, which is in a good state of preservation. The statues depicted the seven Epigonoi, the successors of the Seven against Thebes, who launched a campaign against Thebes, conquered the city and destroyed it. The monument of the Epigonoi has an inscription that simply says 'the Argives dedicated [this] to Apollo'.

Directly opposite this monument, the Argives dedicated another semicircular monument, along with Epanimondas and the Thebans, after the foundation of Messene in 369 BC. This had an exedra revetted with marble, with an inner diameter of 12 m., on which were erected ten statues of ancient kings and queens of Argos: Danaos, Hypermnestra, Lynkeus, Abas, Akrisios, Danae, Perseus, Alektryon, Alkmene, and Herakles. The **monument of the kings**, the work of the sculptor Antiphanes, was erected specifically to give prominence to the alliance between Argos and Thebes at this date and point up the close relationship between the Argives and the Thebans, which was based on the mythological circumstance that it was in Thebes that Alkmene gave birth to Herakles, an Argive by descent. This link helped to achieve the reconciliation being sought by the Argives with the then powerful state of Thebes.

Behind the offerings on the right of the Sacred Way was a large rectangular niche, possibly created in the Hellenistic period. Some scholars once believed that this housed the great dedication of the Spartans, but the view proved to be mistaken, and nothing is known about this particular monument.

In front of the anonymous dedication are the remains of a rectangular pedestal that supported a bronze group depicting Philopoimen, the general of the Achaean League, mounted on horseback and killing the King of Sparta Machanidas at the Battle of Mantineia (207 BC). On the front of the pedestal is a votive inscription that tells us that 'the Achaean League [honours] Philopoimen son of Kraugis, of Megalopolis, for his virtue and goodwill towards them'.

The two statue bases and two niches after the monument of the Argive kings have not been identified with any certainty.

On the left side of the Sacred Way, next to the monument of the Epigonoi, are preserved the remains of the base that bore the **dedication of the Tarentines**, made to commemorate their victory over the Messapioi after 473 BC. The dedication consisted of bronze statues depicting Messapian women prisoners, and horses, and was erected out of the proceeds of the booty from battle. The statues were by the Argive sculptor Agelas, who was active in the early decades of the 5th century BC. Four of the plinths, three of them bearing inscriptions, are still preserved.

The remains next to the dedication of the Tarentines belong to the **Treasury of the Sikyonians**. This was a Doric poros building with two columns *in antis* on the facade. It was built about 500 BC by the oligarchs who overthrew the Orthagorid tyranny of Sikyon. The building material used in the construction of this monument included architectural members taken from two earlier poros buildings erected by Kleisthenes, the tyrant of Sikyon. One of these was a circular tholos, 6.32 m. in diameter and with thirteen Doric columns, which goes back to around 580 BC, and the other was a small monopteral Doric structure, an open pavilion, measuring about 4.2 x 5.50 m. with 4 x 5 columns and adorned with fourteen small rectangular relief metopes. Four of these metopes, which are in a fairly good state of preservation, are now in the museum, and are of great importance to the history of Greek sculpture. This monopteral building probably housed the chariot with which Kleisthenes won his victory at the Pythian games of 582 BC. All that now survives of the Archaic Treasury of the Sikyonians are a few remains of its poros foundation.

1,2. Ruins of the Treasury of the Sikyonians.
3. Poros metope from the Treasury of the Sikyonians.

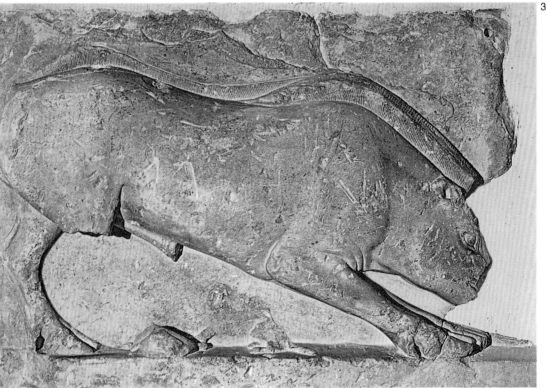

The most beautiful and elegant building in the Delphic sanctuary, in Herodotus' view, was the **Treasury of the Siphnians**. This was built of Parian marble about 525 BC and, according to Pausanias, was erected not to commemorate a victory but rather as a demonstration of the wealth and flourishing economy of Sikyon, being built from a tithe from the profits of the gold mines in this small island. The treasury was a very beautiful Ionic building, some remains of which still survive, and its facade had two Caryatids instead of columns. These supported an entablature with opulent sculptural decoration in the form of a frieze 29.63 m. long and adorned with masterful reliefs encircling the treasury on all four sides, and a pediment. The building had dimensions of 8.55 x 6.12 m. Most of its sculptures that have survived, which are outstanding examples of mature Archaic sculpture, are now on display in the Delphi Museum.

Reconstruction drawing of the facade of the Treasury of the Siphnians.

At the so-called Crossroads of Treasuries the Sacred Way turns sharply right and ascends the hill.

Opposite the treasury of the Siphnians, on the right, are preserved the remains of a poros treasury on which are inscribed many inscriptions in honour of Megarians; this was probably the **Treasury of the Megarians**.

Traces of the terrace wall that supported the treasury of the Boeotians can be seen in the angle formed by the Sacred Way, and in the north-west corner of the sanctuary are preserved traces of the Doric **Treasury of the Thebans**, built after the battle of Leuktra in 371 BC. A stone omphalos was set up in front of this. Nearby are the remains of a small building in which, according to Pausanias, blue schist plinths were placed bearing statues dedicated by the Liparaians, after a victorious naval battle against the Etruscans.

A short distance away are the ruins of a treasury that was probably erected by the Potidaians, and the ruins of another Archaic treasury that has not been identified.

After the turn in the Sacred Way, we come to an important building, the **Treasury of the Athenians**. This is one of the few monuments in the sanctuary that archaeologists have been able to restore. The treasury was fairly well preserved and was restored in 1903-1906 by the Frenchman Replat, at the expense of the municipality of Athens. It is a Doric building with two columns *in antis* on the facade, made of Parian marble, and dedicated to Apollo either after the Battle of Marathon in 490-489 BC or, according to another view, after the restoration of the Athenian democracy in the final decade of the 6th century BC (505-500 BC). It measures 9.68 x 6.62 m. and has thirty metopes decorated with reliefs, and sculptured pediments. The east pediment may have depicted the meeting of Theseus and Peirithoos, and the west probably a battle scene. The twenty-four best preserved of the thirty metopes in the treasury are on display in the museum and are important works for the study of Late Archaic Attic sculpture. Plaster casts of them have been placed on the building. The six metopes on the east side depict scenes of an Amazonomachy, symbolising the victory of the Greeks over the barbarians, while the six metopes on the west side depicted the seizure of the oxen of Geryones by Herakles. The nine metopes on the north side also depicted labours of Herakles and the nine corresponding to them on the south side had scenes of the feats of the Athenian hero Theseus.

Reconstruction drawing of the east facade of the Treasury of the Athenians.

The walls of the treasury are covered with inscriptions incised upon them in the 3rd century BC, most of them honorific decrees in favour of Athenian citizens. Many of these inscriptions are adorned with wreaths, and amongst them are decrees relating to the Athenian *theoria*, decrees concerning the guild of the 'Dionysiac Artists', and two hymns to Apollo, accompanied by musical notation, incised on the sides of the south wall of the treasury. Along the south side of the treasury was a pedestal on which the trophies taken at Marathon were displayed in the open air, as is clear from the large-scale inscription on the pedestal: 'The Athenians [dedicated] to Apollo the spoils taken from the Medes at the battle of Marathon'.

On the other side of the Sacred Way, opposite the Treasury of the Athenians, stands the **Treasury of the Syracusans**, a Doric building which, according to Pausanias, was built by the Syracusans after their victory over the Athenians in Sicily in 413 BC. Next to this are the foundations of the Treasury of the Knidians and Ionic building of Parian marble erected before the capture of Knidos by the Persians in 544 BC.

1

2

1,2. The Treasury of the Athenians.

*3. Part of the Sacred Way with the Treasury of the Athenians at the left, the remains of the Bouleuterion
(Council Chamber) next to it, and part of an Ionic column in front of it.*

Just opposite the treasury of the Athenians are the ruins of **bouleuterion** (council-chamber) of Delphi. This was a long narrow poros building dating from the Archaic period, in which the fifteen councillors and prytaneis of Delphi held their meetings.

Nearby are some of the earliest and most venerable ruins on the site. This was the ancient **sanctuary of Ge**, which is associated with the oracle of Ge and her daughter Themis, and was guarded by the fearsome Python before Apollo made himself master of the site. Here too was worshipped the god Poseidon, who was originally associated with the sea. This sacred precinct is bounded by a circle of large rocks, in turn encircled by an irregular wall enclosing a spring.

A rock nearby, which fell from the Phaidriades thousands of years ago, is said by Pausanias and Plutarch to have been the **Rock of the Sibyl**. It is here that the first Sibyl, who predicted the Trojan War, was thought to have prophesied.

A small rock higher up is the **Rock of Leto**. According to tradition, it was here that Leto stood holding her son Apollo, who was still an infant, while he shot an arrow at the Python and thus made himself master of the site.

The Rock of the Sibyl.

This entire area was destroyed after 548 BC, when work began on preparations for the great temple, and particularly for the construction of the polygonal retaining wall.

On a third rock, the **Sphinx of the Naxians** stood on a tall column, a monument with a total height of 12 m. This offering was made of Naxian marble and was erected about 550 BC. On its base is carved an inscription dating from 332 BC renewing the right of prior consultation of the oracle that had been accorded to the Naxians.

Near the spring in the sanctuary of Ge guarded by the Python, are the remains of an exedra built by the wealthy Athenian sophist Herodes Atticus. Further to the west is a well-preserved small spring, that belonged to a small sanctuary of Asklepios. The temple in this sanctuary was built on the remains of an Archaic treasury attributed by some to the Etruscans.

In front of the Rocks of Cybele and Leto, there were a number of plinths alongside the Sacred Way, amongst which was discovered the pedestal for the **offering of the Boeotians**.

Directly opposite this, the Sacred Way crossed a circular clearing which the ancients called the **Halos**, which was 16 m. in diameter and may once have been encircled by benches. This was an open space used for gatherings. It was here that the Septerion was performed during the Pythian games. This was a morality play concerning the killing of the Python by Apollo. Apollo was played by a boy both of whose parents had to be still alive. The priests, carrying lighted torches, led the boy up a staircase called the Dolonia, to a hut to shoot an arrow at the Python which was supposed to be hiding there. Afterwards the boy fled, supposedly to Tempe to be purified, just as the god Apollo had done. Two ditches containing a wealth of Archaic material were discovered by P. Amandry in 1939.

Around the Halos were other important buildings, including the **Treasury of the Klazomenians,** the **Treasury of the Cyrenaians**, which was probably built between 350 and 325 BC and, to its right, the Prytaneion, which probably stood here. A little higher up are the remains of the Treasury of the Spartan General Brasidas and the Akanthians of Chalkidike. The north-west side of the Halos is bounded by the retaining wall built in 548 BC to support the great temple of Apollo, built by the Alkmeonids. This wall has meticulous polygonal masonry of irregular interlocking blocks. More than 800 official decisions were inscribed on this wall by the ancients, most of them referring to manumissions of slaves between 200 BC and 100 AD.

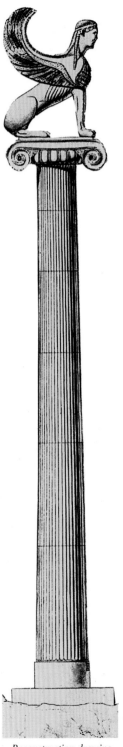

Reconstruction drawing of the Sphinx of the Naxians.

The Temple of Apollo.

Reconstruction drawing of the "Stoa of the Athenians", below the great temple.

In front of this, on the left side of the Sacred Way, the Athenians built an Ionic stoa, probably after 478 BC, to house the trophies taken from the Persians. The **stoa of the Athenians**, which was 30 m. long and only 4 m. deep, stood on a crepis with three steps that supported seven monolithic Ionic columns. These had bases and capitals of Parian marble and in turn supported a timber entablature and the roof.

Public decrees were inscribed on the wall on the back of the stoa. A large votive inscription carved in Archaic letters on the stylobate, tells us 'The Athenians [dedicated] the stoa and the weapons and figureheads, having captured them from the enemy.' According to P. Amandry, this stoa housed the cables from the pontoon bridge constructed across the Hellespont by Xerxes for his army to cross, and various decorative elements from the prows of ships captured after the siege of Sestos. The stoa also housed booty from later Athenian victories, which was brought here later on.

On the right, opposite this stoa, are the ruins of the **Treasury of the Corinthians**. Herodotus attributes this treasury to the Tyrant Kypselos of Corinth (657-628 BC), and it is the earliest treasury at Delphi. It contained a bronze palm-tree standing on the ground covered with snakes and frogs. All the valuable offerings made by the Lydian and Phrygian kings were brought here from the temple of Apollo after it was destroyed by fire in 548 BC.

Before the Temple of Apollo lie the ruins of one of the most venerable dedications at Delphi, the **offering of the Plataians**. A circular pedestal that still survives supported a bronze column formed of three symmetrically intertwined snakes, on top of which was placed a gold tripod.

The dedication was a tithe from the spoils taken by the Greeks from the Persians after the Battle of Plataia in 479 BC. On the sinuous coils Of the snakes were incised the names of the cities that took part in the Battle of Plataia. The gold tripod was seized by he Phokians during the Second Sacred War, and the bronze column was taken off to the Hippodrome in Constantinople by Constantine the Great, where it is still preserved.

In front of the offering of the Plataians can be seen the remains of the second dedication made by the **Tarentines** in the sanctuary. Behind this, near the base of the tripod, stood the offering of the Rhodians, with the gold chariot of Helios, the sun-god, standing on a large base.

Views of the Stoa of the Athenians.

Reconstruction of the acanthus column with the three dancing girls.

Further to the north is a two-storey Doric stoa with eleven columns on the facade, built by Attalos I, the king of Pergamon (241-197 BC). In the 4th century AD, the stoa was converted into a water-system feeding the baths outside the sanctuary enclosure.

Near the stoa of Attalos was the **'oecus of Attalos'** and in front of this a monumental base supporting dedications made by Attalos I, and two taller plinths that bore statues of two kings of Pergamon, Eumenes II and Attalos I.

To the west of the stoa of Attalos are preserved the scant remains of yet another treasury, next to which is a base that probably supported an **offering of the Corcyreans**. Behind the base of the Corcyreans was the **Precinct of Neoptolemos**, the son of Achilles who tradition has it was killed at Delphi by he priests of Apollo and buried at this spot.

Higher up, Pausanias tells us, was a 'not very large stone' on which libations of oil were made every day. Almost directly in front of the Precinct of Neoptolemos is a poros base inscribed with the letters PAN, standing for Pankrates, a famous work-contractor at Delphi. This base bore a high column in the shape of an acanthus leaf that supported a tripod with a bronze cauldron. The cauldron was supported on the head of three beautiful dancing girls or caryatids, which are now on display in the museum. This was a dedication made by the Athenians in the years 350-320 BC.

A long plinth on the left held nine statues, as is evident from the cavities on its surface. This was the **offering of the Thessalian tetrarch Daochos II** who was *hieromnemon* at Delphi in the years 336-332 BC. The nine statues depicted the god Apollo, the dedicator himself, and members of his family. The inscriptions relating to each individual statue can be made out on the front of the pedestal. Next to the monument of Daochos is a horseshoe-shaped base which supported at least seventeen statues of Hellenistic date.

On the Sacred Way are two inscribed bases that supported tripods and figures of Nike made of gold and weighing not less than fifty talents. These were dedications by the tyrants of Syracuse, Gelo and his brother Hiero, which they dedicated in the sanctuary after their victory over the Carthaginians at Himera in 481 BC. To the left are two more inscribed bases that have been identified as dedications by their brothers, Polyzalos and Thrasyboulos.

Further still to the left are more offerings: a large square base that supported the colossal statue of Apollo Sitalkas, which was 15.50 m. high; a pedestal for the **offering of Aristaineta**, which stood on two tall Ionic columns; and the base for the bronze Palm-tree of Eurymedon. This palm-tree supported a gilded statue of the goddess Athena, dedicated by the Athenians after their victory over the Persians at the mouth of the river Eurymedon in the decade 470-460 BC (probably 468 BC).

Behind the foundations of the palm-tree, which are still preserved, is the **monument of Prusias II, the king of Bithynia**. On the pedestal stood a stature of King Prusias on horse-back, which was dedicated by the Aetolian League, according to the inscription incised towards the top of the pedestal. In recent years the precise site of the Kassotis Spring has been identified behind the stele of Prusias. The spring played an important role during the ritual preparations for the issuing of oracles. It was believed that water from the spring bubbled up into the adyton of the Temple of Apollo.

While wandering amongst the monuments, visitors will have become well aware that the building that dominated the site at the height of its glory was the Temple of Apollo.

Column of King Prusias of Bithynia.

The plinths of the tripods dedicated by the tyrants of Sicily can be seen at the bottom left.

In the open area in front of the great temple are preserved the remains of the large altar of the god. The altar, on which the sacrifices were made, was a **dedication by the Chians**, as we are informed by the inscription inscribed towards the top of it: 'The Chians [dedicated] the altar to Apollo'. Another inscription at the foot of the altar refers to the right of prior consultation granted to the Achaeans, who were allowed to receive oracles immediately after the inhabitants of Delphi. The precise date of the dedication is

unknown. All that can be said is that the Chians dedicated the altar to the god during the 5th century BC in gratitude for their delivery. This will be a reference either to the revolt of the Ionian cities against the Persians (499-94 BC), or to the aftermath of the battle of Mykale in 479 BC. The altar, which is 4.60 m. high and 8.58 m. long, was not set precisely on the axis of the temple because it was erected on the site of an earlier altar that stood here before the fire of 548 BC. It was made of black Chian marble, including the three steps, apart from the base and top, for which white marble was used.

In the 2nd century BC a tall column was erected next to the altar to hold the gilded statue of Eumenes II, the king of Pergamon, which was **dedicated by the Aetolians**. A little further along, to the south-west of the altar, rose a tall column supporting an equestrian statue of the Roman General Aemilius Paulus who defeated Perseus, the king of Macedonia, at the battle of Pydna in 168 BC. According to Plutarch, this Hellenistic statue was erected on a 'large square column'. The reliefs of the pedestal are preserved, with scenes of a cavalry conflict between the Macedonians and Romans.

At this point are preserved the ruins of the most important building in the sanctuary, the building that housed the opthalmos, the centre of the world in ancient Greek eyes, and whose renown radiated throughout the entire Greek world: the **Temple of Apollo**.

The surviving temple is he third known from historical times and was built in the 4th century BC. According to legend, the first temple of the god took the form of a hut and was made of laurel leaves brought here from Tempe. The second mythical temple was made of wax and swans' feathers and was built by bees. Finally, the third was made of bronze and was the work of Haephaistos and Athena. The first temple of historical times (the fourth in this series) was of poros and, according to Homer, was built with the aid of the god Apollo by the mythical architects Trophonios and Agamedes. It was a Doric temple, erected on the same site

1. The Altar of the Chians (view from the Sacred Way).

2. View of the Temple of Apollo from the south-west.

as the present structure, and the building remains that have come to light during the excavations suggest that it goes back to the 7th century BC (about 650 BC).

This temple was destroyed by fire in 548 BC. The Amphictyonic League decided to erect a new temple, the costs for the building of which, amounting to three hundred talents, were covered by contributions by the member states of the Amphictyony, donations from all over the Greek world, and generous gifts by foreign rulers. The building of it was undertaken by the great Athenian family of the Alcmeonids, who had been sent into exile by Peisistratos and his sons. The work was completed in 510 BC. This structure, which had dimensions of 59.50 x 23.80 m., was a Doric temple with six columns on the facade and fifteen on the sides. It was a poros apart building from the facade and the sculptures on the east pediment, which were made of marble rather than the cheaper poros envisaged in the contract, and paid for by the Alcmeonids themselves. The east pediment depicted Apollo arriving at Delphi in a four-horse chariot, in which Artemis and Leto were riding at the

right and three kouroi and three kores at the left. This temple, too, was destroyed, by an earthquake in 373 BC. Once again the Amphictyonic League launched an appeal throughout Greece to meet the costs of the new temple.

Work began on the rebuilding of the temple and had probably progressed quite significantly by 356 BC, when it was suspended on account of Third Sacred War.

Despite the interruptions and problems the temple was brought to completion and inaugurated in 330 BC. It was built to the same dimensions and the same design as the previous, Archaic temple, with six columns on the ends and fifteen columns on the sides, and with a pronaos and opisthodomos. The architects were Spintharos of Corinth, followed by Xenodoros and Agathon. Poros coated with stucco was used for the columns and the entablature and dark stone from

1. Remains of the retaining wall supporting the Temple of Apollo.

2. Restored columns from the temple.

3. East side of the sanctuary with the plinth of Prusias of Bithynia at the right.

Parnassos for the rest of the temple. The pedimental sculptures, which were made by the Athenian artists Praxias and Androsthenes, were made of Parian marble. According to Pausanias, the east pediment, like that of the previous temple built by the Alkmeonids, depicted the arrival of the god Apollo at Delphi; the west pediment showed the Sun-god setting and Dionysos amongst the Thyiades, the Delphic name for the Maenads.

2

3

65

The temple metopes were not decorated with reliefs, but had the Persian shields seized at the Battle of Marathon fixed to them, along with shields seized during the raid by the Gauls on Delphi in 279 BC.

Access to the temple was by way of a ramp. Earthquakes and systematic destruction at the hands of Christian fanatics have caused irreparable damage to the temple. The interior may partly be reconstructed thanks to the ancient written sources and those parts of it that have survived. This evidence is insufficient for a complete description, however, and archaeology has not succeeded in fully illuminating the question.

The pronaos of the temple was carved with aphorisms attributed to the Seven Sages, such as 'know thyself', and 'nothing in excess', which advocated a wise, measured, and moral approach to life. There was also a bronze portrait of Homer, on the base of which was inscribed the oracle given to the blind bard.

Above the door between the pronaos and the cella was fixed a capital E on its side, originally made of bronze, though later of gold. The significance of this is still unknown. When Plutarch served as a priest at Delphi, he wrote an entire trea-

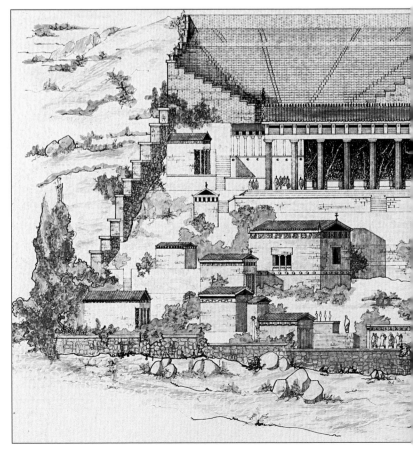

tise attempting to interpret it, though without illuminating the problem.

The cella was divided into two parts. The front contained an altar dedicated to Poseidon, who was the dominant deity in the sanctuary before Apollo, the statues of Zeus Moiragetes and Apollo Moiragetes, the iron throne of Pindar, on which he sat and sang hymns to Apollo, and the hearth on which the priest of Apollo killed Neoptolemos, the son of Achilles. The second part of the cella was the sacred adyton, in which the prophesies revealing the divine will were issued by the Pythia in her state of ecstasy.

In this section was the prophetic chasm, the tripod, the omphalos, and a gold statue of Apollo. It was in the adyton that the water of the Kassotis spring flowed, though the precise arrangement of this is unknown. Pausanias tells us that very few people had the right to enter the adyton. The temple also had an opisthodomos, corresponding with the pronaos. Six of the columns now survive, partly restored with ancient material.

Between the stylobate of the temple and the polygonal wall can be seen the ruins of a small spring and **sanctuary of the Muses**, as well as the remains of some Archaic treasuries. The

Reconstruction drawing of the Temple of Apollo.

ruins of some unidentified Archaic treasuries can also be seen behind the temple.

The **offerings of the Messenians of Naupaktos** stood to the south of the Temple of Apollo on the terrace supported by the polygonal wall. It consists of two figures of Nike standing on triangular bases, which were erected after the victory of the Messenians (fighting on the side of the Athenians) over the Spartans at Spakteria and Pylos in 425 BC.

Reconstruction drawing of the offering of Krateros.

A large retaining wall called the Ischegaon was built to the north of the temple during the 4th century BC (after 356 BC). The name, which means 'earth retainer' is known from inscriptions containing the construction accounts for the temple. It has a partly ruined niche that probably housed a statue.

As visitors continue their tour, they come to the **offering of Krateros** at the west end of the retaining wall. This is large rectangular exedra.

The dedication was made after 320 BC by the son of Krateros, one of Alexander the Great's generals. The exedra housed a group of bronze statues which, according to Plutarch's description, rendered a hunting scene at Susa in Persia, and showed hunting dogs, Alexander the Great wrestling with a lion, and his general Krateros rushing to help him in his difficulties. The son of Krateros, who was himself also called Krateros dedicated the monument after his father's death. The statues were by the great sculptors Lysippos and Leochares. At the back of the exedra, on the wall in the niche, is a verse inscription giving an account of the scene and the name of the dedicator.

Before proceeding to the theatre, it is worth going out through gate C in the sanctuary enclosure wall to see the ruins of a large stoa. This was **dedicated by the Aetolians** from the booty from their victory against the Gauls in 279 BC; it is divided into two by a double colonnade. The stoa was used by pilgrims visiting the sanctuary to rest and shelter from inclement weather. In Roman times the east part of it was converted into a bathhouse.

From the dedication of Krateros a staircase leads up to the **sanctuary theatre**. This is one of the best preserved Greek theatres. It was built in the 4th century BC of white stone from Parnassos, and probably replaced an earlier wooden theatre. The *cavea* (auditorium) included 35 rows of seats divided by a *diazoma* (landing). The upper part of the *cavea* above this landing was accessible from gate E in the sanctuary enclosure wall and was divided into six 'wedges' of seats, while the lower part, to which access was through gate D, was divided by six staircases into seven 'wedges'. The orchestra, 18.5 m. in diameter, is paved and has a channel around it to lead off rain-water. It is clear from the foundations that the stage was divided into two parts: the proscenium at the front, which had three areas, and the stage proper behind it with another three areas. The theatre must have had a reasonable height, though probably did not block the superb panoramic view of the landscape around Delphi.

The Theatre.

According to an inscription, the theatre was restored in 159 BC at the expense of Eumenes II, the king of Pergamon. who in addition to providing the finance, also sent slaves to work on the repairs. In the first century AD a marble relief frieze was placed in front the stage depicting the labours of Herakles. This is now on display in the museum.

The theatre is reckoned to have had a capacity of about 5,000 spectators, and was used mainly for musical and dramatic performances, especially during the major festivals held in the sanctuary. Large numbers of decrees and public decisions are inscribed on the walls all around relating mainly to the manumission of slaves, since the theatre at Delphi served as a meeting place for vast numbers of people.

Just beyond the theatre are the ruins of the **Lesche of the Knidians**. This was a rectangular hypostyle room measuring 18.70 x 9.70 m., which served as a meeting and relaxation room. The roof was supported by eight wooden columns in two rows of four. The entrance on the south side led into the interior of the room, and along the walls there was a continuous bench for the members. The club was dedicated by the Knidians about 460 BC and was famed for its superb wall-paintings, which were by Polygnotos of Thasos, the great painter of the early Classical period.

Reconstruction drawing of the Lesche of the Knidians.

To the right of the entrance was a depiction of the capture of Troy, and to the left Odysseus's descent into Hades. Vase-painters contemporary with Polygnotos borrowed many motifs from the great painter, and these, taken together with the detailed description by Pausanias, give us detailed knowledge of the style and compositions of the Thasian artist.

Finally, to the north-west of the theatre, is the **stadium** of Delphi. This is reached by a path leading up the hill which is well worth the ascent. On the way, they will encounter an ancient spring known by its modern name Kerna. A large number of recesses, which will have held votives, statues, etc., are carved in the rocks around it.

The north side of the stadium was built directly on the Rodini rock, and the entrance was at the east. Here were erected four pillars supporting a triple arch that formed three entrances. The two central pillars had niches for statues.

The stadium was first built in the 5th century BC. An inscription incised on the long stone on the outer side forbade anyone to carry wine outside the stadium on penalty of a five drachma fine. Originally spectators sat directly on the ground but in the reign of the emperor Hadrian, Herodes Atticus paid for the construction of rows of seat made of limestone from Parnassos, not from white marble, as Pausanias reports.

The ancient Theatre.

The stadium is 177.55 m. long, and ranges in width from 25.25 or 25.65 at the ends to 28.50 m. in the middle. The track runs from the starting gates (*aphesis*) at one end to the finish (*terma*) at the other. The starting gates were marked by marble slabs with fluting to give a grip for the runners' feet, and square notches in which were inserted the posts separating the contestants.

The two long sides of the stadium with the seats, forming the 'theatre', were linked by a semicircular *sphendone*, or curve, at the end. The spectators were separated from the track by a tall wall or podium with orthostats as high as 1.30 m. Above the seats a corridor encircled the entire periphery of the theatre to facilitate movement of spectators. This corridor was reached by four staircases. The north side of the stadium had twelve rows of seats, while the *sphendone* and south side had only six, because of the difference in height due to the sloping terrain. The rows of seats were divided by staircases. In the middle of the north side is a long bench with a backrest occupying the width of two rows of seats. These were honorary seats for the judges and officials. At the north-west end of the narrow corridor above the seats was a spring protected by a domed structure, which provided drinking-water for the spectators.

The stadium was used during the Pythian games for the athletic and equestrian contests and possibly also for the music contests before the construction of the theatre. Down to the middle of the 5th century BC, the former events were held in the plain of Krisa. The stadium is reckoned to have held about 7,000 spectators.

Views from the stadium.

THE KASTALIAN SPRING

After visiting the sanctuary of Apollo, we proceed to the sanctuary of Athena Pronaia (Marmaria). On the way we come to the Kastalian Spring. The famous spring is only a few metres from the road, at the foot of Hyanpeia, at the mouth of a wild gorge formed between the two Phaidriades rocks.

The ancient Greeks used to praise the clear crystalline water of Kastalia, which was used for purification purposes when oracles were being issued. Its bubbling waters, were used to sprinkle the great temple of the god. The form of the spring gives clear expression to the creative spirit that overcame the Greeks, urging them to embellish the beautiful things bestowed upon them by nature.

They cut into the rock where the water of the spring bubbles forth, forming a kind of 'chamber' (Chr. Karouzos), with eight steps leading down into it.

Originally the water was collected in a narrow cistern, 0.50 m. wide cut into the base of the rock, with a dam made of stone slabs 2.50 m. high, regulating the level of the water. There were seven spouts set at regular intervals and hidden by bronze lion's heads, from which the water ran. The spouts were separated by eight marble pilasters. After issuing through these water-spouts, the water collected in an open rectangular cistern used for purification before entering the sanctuary of Apollo. On the rock were carved niches in which dedications, statuettes, etc. were placed.

This structure dates from the Hellenistic and Roman periods (possibly the 3rd century BC).

In 1959 the Kastalian Spring of Archaic and Classical times was discovered by chance. It was made of poros and was probably constructed in 600-590 BC, 50 metres below the Hellenistic Spring. It consisted of a paved courtyard surrounded by walls with high orthostates.

There were benches along the side walls, and four bronze lion's head waterspouts were affixed to the north wall, from which the water issued. Pindar's ode undoubtedly refers to this sacred spring and its pure water.

The Kastalian spring, symbol of cleansing and purification.

THE SANCTUARY OF ATHENA PRONAIA

The cult of a female deity was practised on the site of the Sanctuary of Athena Pronaia from as early as the Mycenaean period, as is clear from terracotta female figurines dating from the LH III period discovered there.

From the Archaic period onwards, the site was dedicated to Athena Pronaia, that is the goddess who dwells before the temple, because her sanctuary lay in front of the temple of the great god. Today the site is known as Marmaria. The sanctuary was surrounded by an enclosure wall in which were a number of entrances, the main one at the east. The first remains one encounters are those of altars. Here there stood a large rectangular 6th century altar, with other smaller ones around it. The two built altars hard against the retaining wall were dedicated to Eileithyia (altar on the left) and Hygeia (altar on the right), as we are informed by the inscriptions accompanying them. Nearby are three inscribed stelai, which, again as we learn from inscriptions, were dedicated to Zeus Polieus, Athena Ergane, and Athena Zosteria.

On a higher terrace bounded by retaining walls are preserved the ruins of two temple-shaped buildings with a pronaos and cella, measuring 6.10 x 8 m. and 4.85 x 3.95 m. They probably belonged to the precinct of Phylakes, a hero of Delphi who, together with Autonoos, repelled the Persians in 480. Other scholars regard these Archaic buildings as treasuries.

Next we come to the poros temple of Athena Pronaia. The first temple of the goddess was a peripteral Doric temple built on the same site around 650 BC, which was one of the earliest

Reconstruction drawing of the sanctuary of Athena Pronaia, with the tholos opposite.

monumental temples in Greece. This building was destroyed by falls of rocks from the sides of Parnassos at the end of the 6th century BC, though a number of column drums are preserved and twelve characteristic early Doric capitals that look like 'risen loaves of bread'.

The second Archaic temple was built on the same site about 500 BC. It, too, was a Doric peripteral structure measuring 13 x 28 m. with six columns on the ends and twelve on the side. It had a pronaos with two columns in antis, and a very long cella with no opisthodomos.

Falls of rocks from the Phaidriades during the Persian Wars and in 373 BC caused serious damage to this temple. After the earthquake in 373 BC consolidation work was undertaken on it, and the spaces between the columns at the north-east corner of it were walled up. In March 1905 a terrible storm caused rocks to fall from Hyampeia, destroying twelve of fifteen columns that survived at that time.

To the west of this temple are preserved the remains of two treasuries made of Parian marble, with a pronaos and cella. The larger of the two measures 7.30 x 10.40 m. This is a Doric temple with two columns *in antis* on the facade,

Plan of the sanctuary of Athena Pronaia.

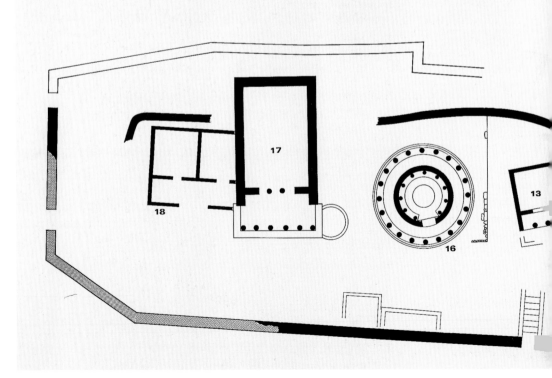

and was built between 480-470 BC. The smaller structure, measuring 6.37 x 8.63 m. is one of the finest examples of the Ionic order surviving from Archaic times. It, too, had a pronaos with two columns *in antis*, and was built by the Massaliotes between 535 and 530 BC. The two columns in antis on the facade had capitals in the rare 'Aeolian' type with palm-leaves. Statues of Roman Emperors were placed inside the cella, on a long pedestal that still survives. A few parts are also preserved of the frieze that adorned the outside walls of the buildings. The beauty and elegance of the Treasury of the Massaliotes rival that of the Treasury of the Siphnians in the Sanctuary of Apollo.

Around the treasuries are bases with cavities in which inscribed stelai were set.

In front of the treasuries stands a large rectangular pedestal, placed obliquely. This held a trophy erected by the people of Delphi in honour of Apollo and Zeus for their assistance in repelling the Persians when they besieged the city in 480 BC.

Next to it is a small pedestal with a statue of the emperor Hadrian, erected by the priest of Apollo, Titus Flavius Aristotimos in AD 125.

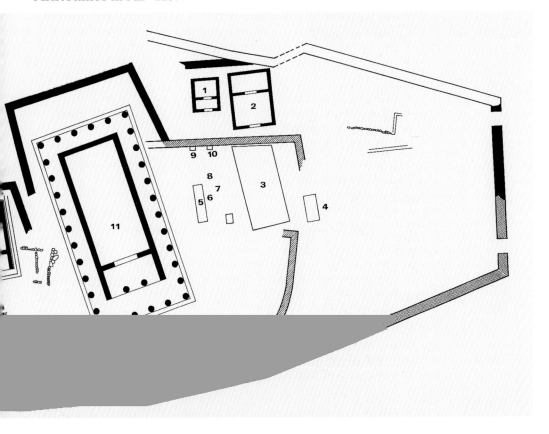

A circular building with three restored columns is preserved to the west of the treasuries. This is the famous tholos, one of the masterpieces of ancient architecture. It was built during the first quarter of the fourth century BC, about 380 BC, the architect being Theodoros from Phokaia in Asia Minor, who also wrote a book devoted to his work. The purpose of the tholos is unknown, though its shape may perhaps point to its having a chthonic character. It is a Doric building with twenty columns supporting the entablature (architrave, triglyphs, metopes, and cornices). The metopes had relief scenes of an Amazonomachy and a Centauromachy.

View of the sanctuary of Athena Pronaia, with the ruins of the Treasury of the Massaliotes in the foreground.

Made of Parian marble, it stood on a crepis with three steps and had a diameter of 13.50 m. The colonnade enclosed the circular cella, the entrance to which was on the south side. The circular wall of the cella had triglyphs and metopes on the outside. Inside, ten Corinthian half-columns stood on a podium made of stone from Eleusis. The relief metopes of the cella depicted the labours of Herakles and Theseus. The base of the wall of the cella was encircled by a superb Lesbian moulding. Finally, the roof had a conical form externally, with marble tiles and akroteria.

To the right of the tholos, in the west of the sanctuary, stands the later temple of Athena Pronaia, which replaced the earlier Archaic temple after it was destroyed by earthquake in 373 BC, as we have seen.

The ancient Greeks decided to build the temple on a different site which was not so exposed to landslides. The new temple, built of grey stone from the quarries at Prophitis Elias near Delphi, was a Doric, prostyle temple with six columns in front of the pronaos and dimensions of 11.55 x 22.60 m.

The pronaos was wider than the cella, and the passageway separating them had two Ionic half-columns *in antis*. The metopes were not decorated with relief scenes. The new temple was built about 370 BC, and its unusual design helps to make it a most beautiful monument.

The last building on the west side of the sanctuary to which visitors come is the **House of the Priests**. This is earlier than the temple and dates from the 5th century BC. It had a prodomos and two rooms, and measured 2.05 x 10.90 m.; its function is not known with certainty.

THE GYMNASIUM

The ruins of the **gymnasium** at Delphi are preserved between the Sanctuary of Athena Pronaia and the Kastalia Spring, close to the bank of the Pleistos. According to legend, it was here that Odysseus was hunting with the sons of Autolykos, when he was wounded in the leg by a boar. When Odysseus returned to Ithaca from Troy, this old wound was recognised by his faithful servant Eurykleia, who knew her master by it.

The young men of Delphi exercised in the gymnasium, and it was here that the athletes trained before the public contests in the stadium during the Pythian games. Because of the sloping site the gymnasium took the form of two long level areas.

On the lower, narrower level were the palaestra, a water cistern for cold baths and thermae for hot baths. The upper level was occupied by the covered *xystos* and a parallel open-air track (*paradromis*) for training in all weathers.

The earliest facilities go back to the Archaic period, but the site received its final form in the 4th century BC and was further repaired in the Roman period.

The palaestra included a central square courtyard surrounded by an Ionic colonnade, in which boxers trained. The north and west sides were given over to various rooms, of which the poros foundations can still be made out. The large room on the west side was used as a changing room.

The first or possibly the third room on the north side was the *konima* or *konisterion*, in which the athletes rubbed themselves with sand. Another of the rooms was

Plan of the Gymnasium.

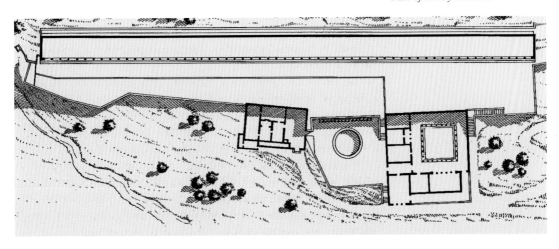

the *sphairisterion*, where boxers and pankratiasts trained with bags full of sand. There was also a temple-shaped room on the west side with two columns *in antis* on the facade, a prodomos, and a main room, at the back of which was a statue of a deity associated with the gymnasium, possibly Hermes or Herakles.

This temple-shaped room was the Ephebeion or Exedra, in which athletes were usually taught by their trainers. In more recent times a church dedicated to the Virgin was built here incorporating a column from the gymnasium, on which Lord Byron and his friend Hobhouse carved their names in 1809.

To the west of the gymnasium was a large courtyard with a circular cistern that was used as a bathhouse. On the retaining wall to the north there were ten basins supplied with water from the Kastalian Spring by eleven spouts above them. The spouts were decorated with bronze animal-muzzles and channelled water into the ten basins, which communicated with each other, and from there to the circular cistern when the athletes were taking their baths.

The thermae for the hot baths were further to the west. They were built by the Romans about AD 120, and had a floor supported on terracotta colonnettes, which allowed hot air to circulate (hypocaust). The *xystos*, on the upper level of the gymnasium, was a large roofed stoa about 7 m. wide. It originally had a poros Doric colonnade in front of it that was replaced in the Roman period by a marble Ionic colonnade.

The distance between the start and finish was a stade (18.443 m.). Alongside it there was an open track called the *paradromis*, where people trained for track events in fine weather, the *xystos* being reserved for training in adverse weather conditions, that is either when it was raining or under a very hot sun.

From the Hellenistic period onwards, the gymnasium was used more generally for cultural events. Important philosophers, poets, musicians, teachers, and so on came here and gave lectures. We also are informed by an inscription that during the Eumeneia, the torch-race started at the gymnasium and ended at the Temple of Apollo.

Views from the Gymnasium.

The Temple of Athena Pronaia.

THE
ARCHAEOLOGICAL
MUSEUM

VESTIBULE

ROOM WITH SMALL FINDS

ROOM OF THE SHIELDS

ROOM OF THE TREASURY
OF THE SIPHNIANS

ROOM OF THE KOUROI

ROOM OF THE BULL

ROOM OF THE TREASURY
OF THE ATHENIANS

ROOMS OF THE
TEMPLE OF APOLLO

ROOM OF THE GRAVE STELAI

THOLOS ROOM

ROOM OF THE
DAOCHOS MONUMENT

ROOM OF THE CHARIOTEER

ANTINOOS ROOM

The Delphi Museum, one of the largest in Greece, houses some of the masterpieces of Ancient Greek Art.

It was originally built in 1902-1903 and was later extended. In it are kept all the finds brought to light at Delphi by the archaeologist's spade, which represent every period of Greek art, and arouse visitors' admiration and astonishment. Over 6,000 exhibits can be seen, reflecting the glory and prestige of the Delphic sanctuary.

The collections of exhibits in the museum rooms are not arranged in chronological order but are grouped according to the place in which they were found.

PLAN OF
THE MUSEUM

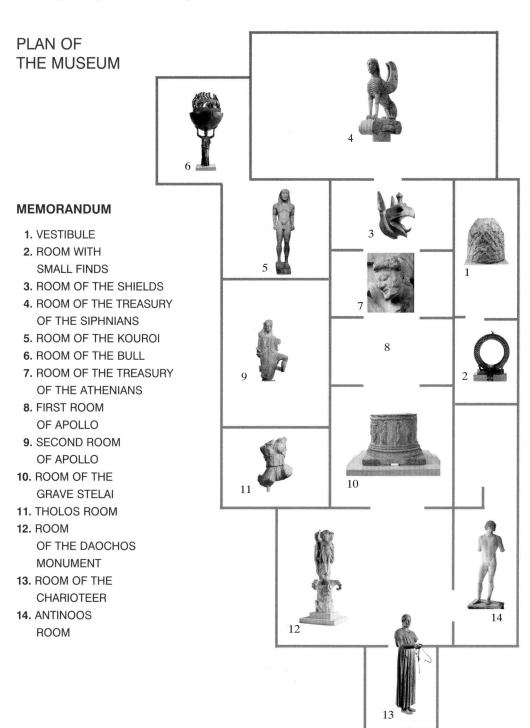

MEMORANDUM

1. VESTIBULE
2. ROOM WITH
   SMALL FINDS
3. ROOM OF THE SHIELDS
4. ROOM OF THE TREASURY
   OF THE SIPHNIANS
5. ROOM OF THE KOUROI
6. ROOM OF THE BULL
7. ROOM OF THE TREASURY
   OF THE ATHENIANS
8. FIRST ROOM
   OF APOLLO
9. SECOND ROOM
   OF APOLLO
10. ROOM OF THE
    GRAVE STELAI
11. THOLOS ROOM
12. ROOM
    OF THE DAOCHOS
    MONUMENT
13. ROOM OF THE
    CHARIOTEER
14. ANTINOOS
    ROOM

VESTIBULE

8194 This is a Hellenistic or Early Roman copy of the famous Delphic omphalos, the most important cult object found at Delphi. Pausanias saw it in front of the Temple of Apollo in the 2nd century AD, and this is where it was actually found. There was also an omphalos inside the adyton of the Temple of Apollo, near the statue of the god. In the Classical period it symbolised the centre of the earth. According to tradition it was a grave marker for the Python, whom the god killed in order receive the oracle. It is made of marble covered with a relief net of woven bands called the *agrenon*. Two gilded eagles were placed on or next to the omphalos.

9467 An iron tripod similar to the one in the adyton of the Temple of Apollo has been placed next the omphalos.

It is surmounted by a cauldron, which, however, does not belong to the tripod and is not even of the same date, but has been placed here to give an idea of the original. **2707** To the left of the omphalos is displayed a marble relief depicting Athena, the omphalos and Apollo. It dates from 330 BC and is the upper part of an honorary stele inscribed with a decree in honour of the great Athenian orator Demades.

2544 Parts of the marble frieze of the theatre proscenium, which dates from the 1st century AD, are exhibited along the wall of the narrow corridor. It has the following relief scenes, from left to right:

a) Herakles in the Garden of the Hesperides.

b) Kerberos. Herakles and the Lion of Nemea.

c) Herakles wrestling with a Centaur.

d) Herakles fighting the Lernaian Hydra.

e) Herakles and Antaios.

2a

f) Scene from an Amazonomachy
   and Herakles wearing the lion-skin headdress.
g) The triple-bodied monster Geryones.
h) Herakles taming the horse of Diomedes.
i) Herakles fighting Diomedes, son of Ares.
j) Herakles and the Stymphalian Birds.
   The next room contains exhibits
dating mainly from the Archaic period.
The tour of this room follows an
anti-clockwise direction.

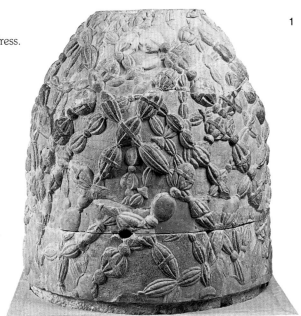

1

1. The Delphic omphalos.
2. Parts of the marble frieze from the Theatre
   A) Herakles fighting the Lernaian Hydra
   and the giant Antaios.
   B) Herakles taming the horses of Diomedes.

2β

ROOM WITH SMALL FINDS

Case 1

The first showcase contains gold, bronze and terracotta jewellery found at Amphissa and dating from the 8th-7th century BC, and also Corinthian and Protocorinthian vases dating from the 8th and 7th-6th century BC found in tombs at Amphissa and at Delphi.

Case 2

The second case contains vases from Delphi dating from the Geometric period (900-700 BC).

Case 3

In the third case we may note the anthropomorphic and zoomorphic figurines dating from the Geometric period (900-700 BC) and parts of bronze tripods of the 8th century BC.

Case 4

In the fourth case visitors will see inlaid figures of Sirens, griffins, lions, etc., and cooking-pots and other bronze vessels of the 8th-7th century.

Case 5

The fifth case is devoted mainly to bronze figurines and statuettes of gods ranging from the Archaic to the Hellenistic period. Items of particular interest here include the bronze statuette of a youth dating from the early Classical period, and other objects of minor art of the 7th and 6th centuries BC.

Case 6

In the 6th case are exhibited parts of bronze vases and vessels from various periods. We may note the bronze bowl with repoussé decoration.

Case 7

This case contains weapons and various votive bronzes from the sanctuary of Apollo, including bronze helmets, axes, spear-heads, decorative plaques, etc.

Case 8

In the eighth case, to the left of the entrance, are displayed clay vases and figurines from a sanctuary at Kirrha (6th-4th century BC). We may note the closed kylix, the upper part of which is decorated with banquet scene and which has Dionysiac scenes between the handles; this is an example of the Severe Style. To the left of the vestibule is the room of the bronze shields.

1. Bronze cauldron handle (8th c. BC).

2,3. Sirens: decorative appliqués
from cauldrons.

4. Bronze figurine of a sheep with Odysseus tied
beneath its belly (6th c. BC).

ROOM OF THE SHIELDS

This room houses some of the finest examples of 7th century BC art. On the walls visitors will see bronze shields that go back to the first half of the 7th century BC.

7226 The first, which is decorated with repoussé concentric circles interrupted by chevrons, was dedicated in the sanctuary of Apollo.

7227, 7177 The other two have a lion's head at the centre surrounded by other animals such as rams, deer, etc.

7734, 8396 Other representative pieces are two protomes of bronze griffins, one hammered and the other cast, that were used as appliqués on cauldrons (7th and 6th century BC).

2527 A small bronze kouros of the so-called 'Daidalic' style dating from the second half of the 7th century BC.

5733 A marble perirrhanterion restored with plaster, which dates from the from the beginning of the 6th century BC. It consisted of three korai around a column supporting the marble basin.

*1. Bronze statuette of a kouros
   in the Daidalic style (640-630 BC).*

*2. Bronze statuette of a youth, known
   as the 'Apollo with the necklace' (525 BC).*

3. Bronze shield with concentric circles.

4. Bronze head of a griffin (70-650 BC).

ROOM OF THE TREASURY OF THE SIPHNIANS

The next room houses some of the finest masterpieces of mature Archaic Ionian art, the outstanding pieces being the superb reliefs that adorned the Treasury of the Siphnians. This building, which dates from about 525 BC, was the most brilliant monument in the sanctuary of Apollo. It embodies the supreme moment of sculpture, and exhibits a tendency for some of the main architectural members to be replaced, with the two Caryatids of the pronaos, for example, functioning as two Ionic columns.

In the right part of this room, the gaze is arrested by the marble winged Sphinx dedicated by the Naxians in the sanctuary of Apollo, which goes back to 570-560 BC. It stood on an Ionic column with six drums and rested on an Ionic capital. The total height of the dedication was about 12.5 m., while the Sphinx itself was 2.32 m. The column had 44 flutes, and the base is inscribed with a decree passed by Delphi renewing the right of prior consultation of the oracle for the Naxians in the year 328/327 BC.

The Sphinx is a representative example of Archaic Naxian art, which coincided with the political domination of the island over the Cyclades and its general prosperity at this time (7th-6th century BC).

The female head with the characteristic Archaic smile, reflects the a more general tendency to humanise such figures. The linear modelling of the breast and wings, and the details, which were once picked out by colour, produce an impressive work that may have been erected in the sacred sanctuary to protect the oracle of Ge, which was formerly guarded by the Python. The two Doric colonnettes behind the sphinx go back to the end of the 6th century BC.

The room is dominated by the sculptural decoration from the Treasury of the Siphnians. This small Ionic building affords the most brilliant example of a consummately conceived and executed frieze. Scholars have recognised the style of at least two artists, though their names are unknown. One, the earlier, worked on the west and south sides and the other the north and east sides.

The first sculptor is the more conservative, and his art reflects the Ionian tradition evolved in the workshops of the Asia Minor coast.

The second must have been a very great artist in his day, as is clear from his bold conception and unique inspiration. He was probably inspired by Chian art, though he moved on from this. His compositional and narrative manner exhibit a rare agility with regard to the object of the composition, and he has produced unrivalled works imbued with great sculptural power, force and expressiveness that do not detract in the slightest from the elegance of the architectural member that they adorned.

1. Head of a caryatid.
2. The Sphinx of the Naxians.

The **east frieze** of the treasury is displayed to the left of the entrance. It depicts the Trojan War, watched by the Olympian gods. The assembled gods are seated and are divided between the two rival camps. At the left are depicted the gods favourably disposed towards the Trojans, towards whom they turn. The first god is Ares, the god of war, seated fully armed at the end. He is followed by Aphrodite (or Leto), Artemis and Apollo, who are engaged in discussion, with Apollo turned towards Artemis. They have characteristic gestures indicating the familiarity between them and giving expression to their profound unease and tension. The next figure, the head of which is not preserved, is Zeus, seated on a throne adorned with a relief scene of a Satyr chasing a Nymph. Thetis, the mother of Achilles, was depicted in front of him in a posture of supplication; the remains of her fingers survive, touching Zeus's knee.

At the right were depicted the gods who supported the Greeks, facing left: Poseidon (who is not preserved), Athena, Hera and Demeter (or Hebe). The section of the frieze depicting the fighting between Greeks and Trojans outside the walls of Troy has the following scenes: at the left a Trojan chariot pulled by four horses, with its charioteer Glaukos. Next come Aeneas and Hector, who have descended from their chariot and are fighting against Menelaos (holding a shield with a gorgoneion) and Ajax, over the body of a dead warrior (Euphorbos?). At the right is a Greek chariot with its charioteer Automedon, and Nestor, urging on the Greeks with his right arm raised.

Treasury of the Siphnians:
1. Part of the scene at the left of the east frieze,
*   with Leto or Aphrodite, Artemis and Apollo.*
2. Right part of the Gigantomachy on the north frieze.
3. South part of the north frieze, with Hermes
*   and Ares fighting giants.*

2

3

The **north frieze** is displayed along the left wall. The subject of this is the battle of the gods and giants. Hephaistos is shown at the left wearing a short chiton, working at his bellows.

He is followed by two goddesses wearing hoplite armour and fighting against two giants. In front of these is Cybele riding on a chariot pulled by two lions which are pulling down a giant. Herakles is fighting with a giant in the background behind her. The next figures are Apollo and Artemis who are shooting their arrows at three giants, while the giant Kantharos is running panic-stricken to the right. His helmet has a crest in the shape of the ancient vase known as a kantharos. Between the two fighting groups lies the body of Ephialtes. Further along is the figure of Zeus on his chariot (which is not preserved) being attacked by two giants. In the foreground, Hera spears a fallen giant and further to the right Athena fights with the giant Laertes, while another giant has fallen to the ground. Next, the bearded Ares fights with two giants (Biatas and Enaphas), beyond which Hermes, holding a sword, attacks two more giants. Finally, parts are preserved of Poseidon and possibly Amphitrite, fighting against two giants.

In this part of the frieze, the sculptor left his name incised on the shield of the third giant against whom Apollo and Artemis are fighting, but it has not survived. This is undoubtedly the most brilliant section of the frieze from the treasury.

On the wall opposite the entrance is displayed the **west frieze**. The theme of this section was the Judgement of Paris, but very few relief figures have survived from it.

According to legend, Peleus and Thetis failed to invite the goddess Eris (Strife) to their wedding, and to take revenge she threw a golden apple amongst the assembled guests inscribed with the words 'the most beautiful'. This led to rivalry between Hera, Aphrodite, and Athena, and to resolve the issue Zeus appointed Paris judge who duly gave the apple to the most beautiful of them, Aphrodite. On the frieze, Hermes is depicted at the left as the charioteer of the winged chariot of Athena, who is also winged and is climbing up into the quadriga. The figure behind her is Hephaistos or Poseidon. The victorious goddess, Aphrodite, was shown at the centre getting out of her chariot and fastening a necklace around her neck. She is undoubtedly the finest relief figure in the entire

frieze. The right part of the frieze is not preserved, but the third goddess, Hera, will undoubtedly have been depicted here with her chariot.

The **south frieze**, the most fragmentary of them all, is displayed to the right. The few preserved pieces reveal a scene of a female figure being abducted, followed by a chariot in front of an altar, and finally two horses and a third chariot. It is not easy to identify these figures, and the subject of the scene has not been established with any certainty. It may have represented the abduction of the daughters of Leukippos by the Dioskouroi, though some see in it the abduction of Oinomaos's daughter Hippodameia by Pelops. Towards the top of the wall on which the frieze with the Battle of the Giants is displayed are two sections of water-spout from the roof of the treasury of the Siphnians. The one at the left is decorated with relief anthemia and lotus flowers, while that at the right has an additional lion's head in the centre.

To the left of the sphinx of the Naxians is one of the two Caryatids that adorned the facade of the Treasury of the Siphnians. The larger part of her body is preserved together with the head and the polos on which the column capital rested. The

kore stood on a tall base and will have worn inlaid metal jewellery on her head, as is clear from the holes in her ears and hair, where a diadem would have been set; this jewellery will have supplemented the serene beauty of her face, with its characteristic Archaic smile. She wore a delicate chiton and heavier, richly draped himation. On the polos she wears on her head is preserved a relief scene of a Nymph or Mainad, a Silenos seizing a Mainad, and a few parts of another relief Silenos.

The column capital supported on the polos is displayed on a tall pedestal in this room, and has a relief of a deer being torn apart by two lions.

To the right of the Sphinx of the Naxians is exhibited a head of a kore. This used to be attributed to the Treasury of the Knidians, but recent research has shown that it should be assigned to the Treasury of the Siphnians and belonged to the second kore adorning its facade. The eyes are oblique and have inlaid stones, and this second head has some significant stylistic differences from that of the previous kore. The cylindrical polos has reliefs of Apollo and his lyre, with four Nymphs depicted next to him, and three Graces and Hermes playing the pipes of Pan in front of him.

Behind the better-preserved of the Caryatids from the Treasury of the Siphnians are the remains of the highly elaborate doorway of the entrance to the cella. This has excellent floral decoration with relief amthemia, lotus flowers, and rosettes, and is comparable to the wonderful surviving doorway of the Erechtheion on the Athenian Acropolis, which is a fine example of the trends and potential of the Ionic order.

To the right of the doorway of the treasury are parts of a building dating from the last quarter of the 6th century BC, which probably housed a valuable dedication in the Archaic temple of Apollo and was decorated with an Ionic moulding,

2

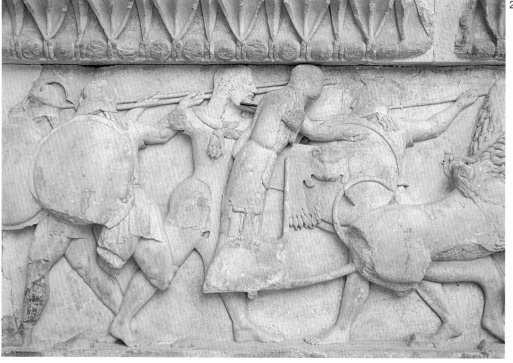

an astragal, anthemia, etc. The Aeolian capital on display belongs to the Treasury of the Massaliotes In the sanctuary of Athena Pronaia, and consequently dates from about 530-510 BC.

The remains of a kore on display to the right of the capital from the Treasury of the Siphnians have been identified as a Caryatid from the Treasury of the Knidians.

Finally, the east pediment of the Treasury of the Siphnians is displayed above the east frieze. It is the only surviving pediment of the treasury and is 0.73 m. at its highest. It depicted a very popular subject in Archaic art, the contest between Herakles and Apollo for the Delphic tripod. According to legend, Herakles seized the prophetic tripod with the aim of founding his own oracle after the Pythia had refused to issue him an oracle because he had not undergone purification for the murder of Iphitos.

The central group shows Herakles at the right holding the Delphic tripod on his shoulder, while Apollo at the left attempts to take it from him. Artemis (or Leto) attempts to restrain the angry Apollo. Between Herakles and Apollo stands the figure of a deity who is attempting to separate them, who has been identified with Athena (or Zeus). Behind Apollo, two female figures stand in front of a chariot, the groom of which is depicted kneeling in the left corner of the pediment. Two figures in the chariot are also shown behind Herakles.

Treasury of the Siphnians.
1. East pediment, depicting the contest between Herakles and Apollo for the Delphic tripod.
2. Part of the scene on the north frieze.
3. Bust of a Caryatid.

ROOM OF THE KOUROI

Visitors now proceed to the Room of the Kouroi. Their attention is at once arrested by the two gigantic statues of the Argive twins Kleobis and Biton carved by the Argive sculptor, Polymedes. These were dedicated by their fellow citizens in the sanctuary at Delphi, near the treasury of the Athenians. The two Archaic statues, carved from Parian marble, take the form of the Archaic kouros combined with the characteristic features of Argive sculpture at this period, and are of unique artistic value.

Herodotus has preserved to us the legend that at the festival of the Heraia, the mother of the twins, who was priestess of Hera, needed to go urgently to the sanctuary of the goddess outside Argos. The oxen pulling her chariot were moving very slowly, so the two youths roped themselves to it and pulled their mother from Argos to the Heraion, a distance of 45 stades (about eight km.). Their mother, proud of her children and pleased with the praise heaped on them by the Argives, prayed to the goddess to grant them 'the finest thing that could befall a human being'. Her prayer was heard by the goddess and the two brothers went to sleep happy that night in the sanctuary and never awoke, thus meeting with the sweetest death.

To honour the two brothers, the Argives dedicated statues of them at Delphi 'for being the best'. The statues are 2.16 m. high and date from 600-580 BC, marking the transition from the Daidalic style of the 7th century to the Archaic art of the 6th century BC. The statues are solid and severe, though the modelling exudes the vigour and dynamism of their bodies. The muscles are sturdy and robust, the waist tight, and the joints full of power and tension. The well-built, robust bodies are surmounted by square heads with a narrow forehead and wide-open eyes, in which can be seen the impetuosity and vigour of the athletes. The sculptural conception and rendering reveal a confident control of space. The volumes are outlined from some inner compulsion and fundamental belief on the part of the sculptor who carved them.

The two marble sculptures are without doubt amongst the finest exhibits in the Museum.

On the left wall of this room are displayed five of the total of fourteen poros metopes from the early treasury of the Sikyonians, known as the monopteral building (pavilion). Exceptionally these were rectangular (88 x 58 cm.) rather than square, and they date from 560 BC. The motifs on the metopes are all admirably self-contained, and they form typical examples of the art of the wealthy, powerful city of Sikyon in Archaic times. Traces of the paint are still preserved and the metopes are distinguished by a pronounced linear tendency.

The metopes are described below from left to right.

The first metope has a subject drawn from the Argonaut expedition, which depicts the front part of the Argonaut's ship (the Argo), showing Orpheus and another figure standing and playing the lyre in order to calm the waves, while the Dioskouroi (Kastor and Polydeukes) disembark from the Argo on their horses.

The second metope depicts the abduction of Europa by Zeus. According to the myth, the god transformed himself into a bull, on to which the beautiful Phoenician princess climbed, and was then carried off from Phoenicia to Crete. Europa is shown leaning forward and clinging to the neck of the galloping bull.

1. The Calydonian boar, reconstruction of the fourth metope from the Treasury of the Sikyonians.
2. The two Archaic kouroi of Kleobis and Biton.

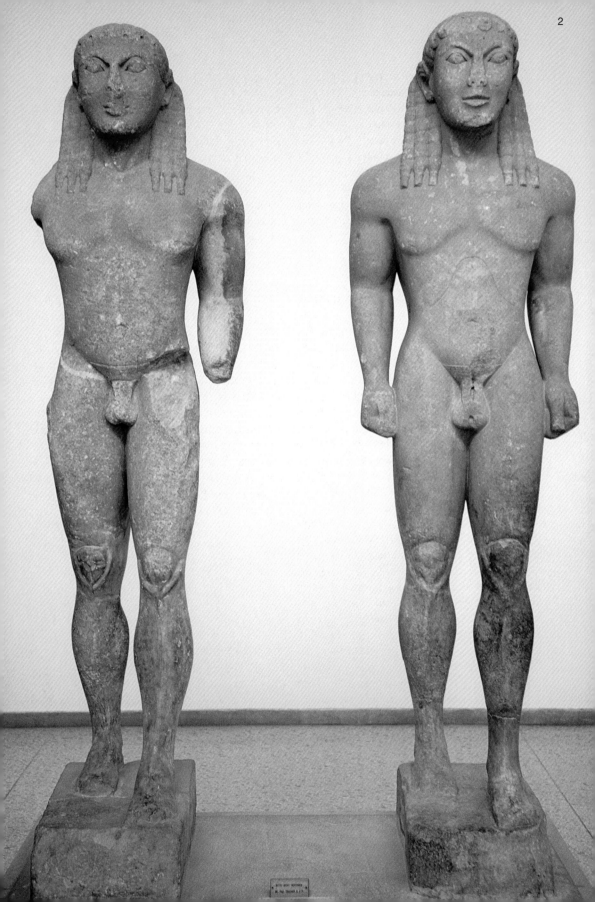

The third and best-preserved metope shows the capture of the cattle by the Dioskouroi, Kastor and Polydeukes, and their cousins, Idas and Lynkeus, the sons of Aphareus. The artist appended the name of each figure, and emphasised it with paint (the name of Lynkeus is missing).

The fourth metope depicts the hunt for the Calydonian boar. The hunt for this fearsome beast was organised by Meleagros, son of the king of Calydon. The remains of one of Meleagros's dogs are preserved beneath the relief figure of the bull.

Finally, the fifth metope, which is badly damaged, shows Phrixos riding on a ram and carrying off the golden fleece.

The figures on the metopes are clear and motionless, accurately drawn, and attain considerable expression through the linear modelling. The episode from the Argonaut expedition is admirably treated as a self-contained subject, and the artist exhibits considerable assurance in its execution.

1663 A small bronze kouros on display on the right side of the room possibly depicts Apollo. He is naked, wears sandals, and has a necklace around his neck. The figure reflects the trends of 'Lakonian art' and dates from 530-520 BC.

The Dioscuri and the sons of Aphareus. The third metope from the Treasury of the Sikyonians.

ROOM OF THE BULL

This room, a continuation of the Kouros Room, is devoted to the material discovered in two deposits beneath the Sacred Way, opposite the treasury of the Athenians, which is presented in a narrative fashion. The deposits were discovered in 1939 by P. Amandry, during his excavation designed to elucidate the pavement of the Sacred Way. It was quite common for the ancient Greeks to gather together earlier, possibly destroyed, objects, dedications, sculptures, etc., and place them in deep pits. These pits (bothroi) not only revealed the care shown by the ancient Greeks for their cult objects, but also protected them from any likely profanation.

The deposits in the Delphic sanctuary contained fragments of dedications made of precious materials such as gold, silver, bronze, ivory, etc. These rich finds are displayed in this room.

1

Case 1

The most important exhibits in the first case are, from the left: a bronze statuette of a flute player (early 5th century), a group of two sphinxes with a single head made of ivory (6th century), a silver kylix, silver and bronze bowls, bronze plaques with repoussé and engraved scenes, and other objects dating from the 5th century BC.

Case 2

In the second case we may note: an ivory statuette of a god brandishing a spear, dating from the early 7th century BC, who has vanquished a panther or a lion; bronze arrowheads, and spear-butts; two bronze Sirens, and bronze plaques that may have been the sheathing of a column capital.

Case 3

The third case contains a partial restoration of a chryselephantine statue of a god seated on a throne and holding a gilded silver bowl in his right hand. This is an Ionic work of the 6th century BC. Also displayed here are two gold plaques that adorned the gods garments, with symmetrical repoussé scenes of animals, the gold diadem worn by the god, the ivory feet, part of the decoration of his throne, including gold cutouts fixed to bronze plaques, and the gold tresses from his head. The case also contains parts of the god's arm, made of ivory, a necklace with gold lion's heads, gold plaques with repoussé decoration, etc.

2

1. Ivory statuette of a man
   and a wild animal.
2. Peplophoros holding a bronze
   incense-burner in her hands.

Gold-and-ivory heads of a man (below)
and Artemis (opposite page).

Hammered statuette of a silver bull (600-550 BC).

Case 4

The fourth case contains the preserved parts of two female chryselephantine statues, possibly depicting Artemis and Leto. Visitors may see the ivory head of Artemis (?) wearing a gold diadem and gold jewellery, the goddess's arm, made of ivory and wearing a gold bracelet, and gold tresses from her hair. Also on display is the head of Leto, made of ivory, her toes, also of ivory, gold bracelets, and two ivory legs that probably belonged to other figures.

Case 5

In the fifth case are displayed works of minor art such as terracotta female figurines, preserved parts of chryselephantine statuettes, a large number of items from the applied decoration of wooden furniture dating from the 6th century BC, and ivory parts from groups of figures; these include scenes of fighting during the Trojan War or the famous group of the Harpies, pursued by Zetes and Kalais, which is an outstanding example of Corinthian miniature art dating from about 570 BC.

Case 6

The sixth case also contains objects of minor art, such as small ivory plaques with fine decoration, ivory groups of figures, vase handles, iron spear-heads, small gold objects, etc.

The back of the room is dominated by the large case containing the silver life-sized bull. This is an outstanding work of Archaic Ionian art dating from the 6th century BC, which was destroyed during the 5th century BC by some unknown cause. It is a precious dedication measuring 2.61 x 1.46 m., which was made entirely of hammered silver plaques connected by bronze bands and nailed to a wooden skeleton with silver nails. It must have been a very impressive dedication, with the horns and other parts of the body gilded.

Finally, a bronze incense-burner set on a separate pedestal is a superb work of art of the mid 5th century BC; it depicts a young woman wearing a peplos and holding a small hemi-spherical bowl for the incense above her head with her upraised arms.

1. Ivory relief.

2. Gold plaques and cutouts with a griffin and a gorgoneion from the statue of Artemis.

2

ROOM OF THE TREASURY OF THE ATHENIANS

The following room houses the reliefs from the treasury of the Athenians, built after the victory at Marathon in 490/89 BC.

Of the thirty metopes that adorned the treasury, nine on the long sides and six on the short, twenty-four are displayed in this room. The metopes provide important evidence for the study of Attic sculpture in the late Archaic period; five or six artists have been recognised as working on them, representing two groups with different stylistic features: one of these was more conservative and followed the traditional Archaic codes, producing figures that were tightly modelled and had an innate vigour; the second was more progressive and succeeded in blending the dictates of Archaic art with a refreshing conception of details, new features, and great elegance. In terms of subject and sculptural quality, the results were figures that served as models and became part of the legacy of the Greek art in general in the Classical period.

The surviving metopes from the nine on the north side of the treasury, which depicted the labours of Herakles, are displayed on the sides of the room to the left and right of the entrance. From right to left, the scenes are: Herakles vanquishing the centaur, Herakles defeating Kyknos, the son of Ares, Herakles with the Kerynian hind, and Herakles with the Nemean lion. The two metopes at the ends have scenes of warriors. The next five metopes to the left depict the tenth labour of Herakles, his fight with the triple-bodied giant Geryones, and the seizure of his oxen (west side of the treasury).

Metope from the north side of the Treasury of the Athenians.

1. Detail of Theseus and Antiope shown in phot. 3.

2. Detail of Herakles from a depiction of Herakles and Kyknos, also from the treasury of the Athenians.

3

The final metope on this side of the room and the six opposite adorned the south side of the treasury, which was the side most readily visible from the Sacred Way. The total of nine metopes depicted the feats of the Athenian hero Theseus. From right to left may be recognised: Theseus with the fearful robber Procrustes, Theseus with the robber Kerkyon, Theseus with a robber, possibly Skiron, and finally, Theseus standing in front of his patron goddess, Athena. The next three metopes depict Theseus with the bull of Marathon, Theseus with Antiope, queen of the Amazons, and finally, the hero with the fearful Minotaur.

The last six metopes in this room adorned the east side, that is the façade, of the treasury. They have scenes from an Amazonomachy that were propaganda for the victories won by Greeks over barbarians and, by extension, the superiority of the restraint, morals, and virtue over irrational, primeval, barbaric nature.

This room also contains remains of the two pediments from the treasury. The east pediment depicted the meeting of Theseus and Peirithoos in front of a deity, and the west a battle scene, with Herakles and Telamon fighting against Laomedon, the king of Troy and father of Priam.

Herakles and the Kerynian hind, with a detail of Herakles opposite.

ROOMS OF THE TEMPLE OF APOLLO

The first and most important exhibit in this room consists of parts of two hymns in honour of Apollo which were inscribed on the south wall of the Treasury of Athenians, accompanied by musical notation. The hymns were probably sung for the first time at the Athenian Pythaids in 138 and 128 BC. Attempts were made to decipher the musical notation by the Germans Bellermann and Fortlage.

The room also contains the remains of the west poros pediment of the Archaic temple of Apollo built by the Alkmeonids. The subject depicted on the pediment was a Gigantomachy, that is the war between the Olympian gods and the giants. The pediments of the temple are believed to have been the work of the famous Athenian sculptor Antenor.

The solid, severe figures exude a monumental quality consistent with the achievements of the art of their time. Amongst the preserved parts may be made out a fallen giant, Athena entering battle, parts of the breasts of two horses, and so on.

Next to these is displayed a small marble kouros

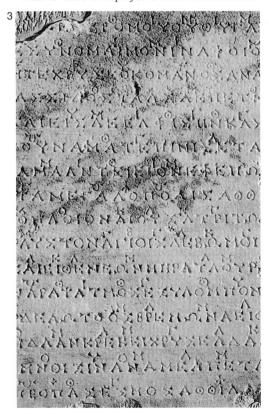

with the head missing, which dates from the early 5th century BC. To the right of it is a headless female statue made of Parian marble, depicting a woman wearing a peplos; this may have been an akroterion from the Doric treasury in the sanctuary of Athena Pronaia. It dates from 470 BC.

In this room are displayed the sculptures from the east marble pediment of the Archaic temple of Apollo, built by the Alkmeonids. The pediment depicts the 'epiphany' of the god - that is, his arrival at Delphi in a four-horse chariot. The centre of the composition is dominated by the god's chariot, in which his sister Artemis and mother Leto are also riding. At the right is depicted Poseidon's son Delphos, the lord of the land, welcoming the god, and two more male figures. The three daughters of Kekrops, Pandrosos, Erse, and Aglauros, are shown at the left. In addition to the standing, frontal figures flanking the god, the corners have groups of lions pulling down animals, with a lion tearing apart a hind at the right and at the left a lion killing a bull.

Details of the sculptures, such as the blood in the wounds, were picked out by paint.

4

To the right of the pediment is displayed a marble winged Nike, which was the central akroterion of the Alkmeonid temple, a marble water-spout from the temple, ending in a lion's head, and a marble kouros dating from 555-540 BC.
To the left of the pediment are displayed a headless Sphinx that was one of the corner akroteria of the Archaic temple, part of a water-spout from the temple built in the 4th c. BC, and another marble kouros dating from 540-520 BC.
The following exhibit in this room is a small bronze cow, which was an offering to Apollo, dating from 500 BC.
This is followed by an Ionic colonnette of Parian marble that served as the base for a dedication by the sons of Charopinos (middle of the 6th c. BC). A kouros, of which only the inscribed base survives, was also dedicated by Charopinos's sons.
Opposite the east pediment are displayed 4 stelai carved with inscriptions dating from 361-310 BC. These refer to the accounts of the city of Delphi for the construction of the temple of Apollo after the fire of 373 BC, and include lists of the cities and private individuals who made contributions towards its reconstruction and the fines imposed on the Phokians after the Third Sacred War.
Above the entrance to the room is a large inscription referring to a repair of the temple of Apollo during the reign of Domitian, in AD 84.

1. Decorative detail.
2. Water-spout of the 4th c.BC.
3. Part of the south wall of the Treasury of the Athenians inscribed with hymns in honour of Apollo.
4. Winged Nike.

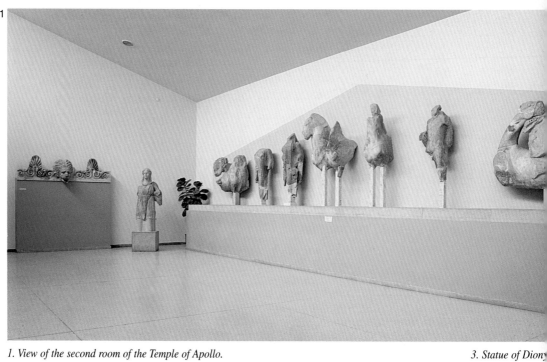

1. View of the second room of the Temple of Apollo.

2. The east pediment of the Temple of Apollo.

3. Statue of Diony

ROOM OF THE GRAVE STELAI

This important room contains part of a grave stele depicting a man wearing a heavy himation, dating from the late 6th century BC, a cinerary urn of the 5th century BC, and three terracotta masques of Demeter or Kore, also dating from the 5th century BC.

The left of the room is dominated by the masterful Early Classical grave stele from the east cemetery at Delphi. It depicts a youthful athlete cleansing his body with a strigil after a wrestling match. In front of him stands his servant holding the aryballos containing oil, and between them is preserved the head of the dead man's favourite dog. The head of the young athlete and his legs from the shins down are missing. This grave stele made of Parian marble is a superb work of an Ionian workshop and the finest object in this room.

Other exhibits in the room worth noting are part of a grave stele depicting a young servant girl holding her mistress's mirror (middle of the 5th century BC), and part of a grave monument with a scene of a young servant holding a round container and accompanying his master to the palaestra, which dates from the first half of the 5th century BC.

A separate showcase is devoted to vases discovered in tombs dating from the 5th century BC, amongst them lekythoi, alabastra, ampho-riskoi, etc.

The second part of the room contains a broken statue of the second half of the 4th century BC. According to one view, this depicts Dionysos and was the central figure in the west pediment of the temple of Apollo (4th century BC).

The tender youthful figure of the god with his gentle gaze accords with the achievements of the art of this period. This exhibit may now have been moved to the room of the Daochos monument.

A second headless statue, dating from the beginning of the 3rd century BC, depicts Apollo playing the kithara. The front part of a horse dating from the 5th century BC, displayed on the wall, was probably part of a scene of a four-horse chariot.

Finally, the circular marble altar almost 1 m. high in the corner comes from the sanctuary of Athena Pronaia and dates from the 1st century BC. It has a relief depiction of twelve young girls with raised arms, hanging pairs of bands decorated with garlands of leaves.

1

1. Circular altar from the precinct of Athena.

2. Grave stele with a relief of an athlete.

2

THOLOS ROOM

1,2. Amazons from the metopes outside the tholos.

*3,4. Female figure from the akroterion
the tholos, and part of the metope.*

124

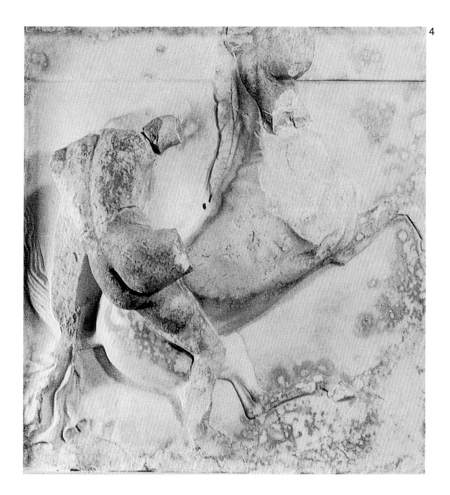

This room houses part of the entablature of the tholos (380-375 BC), the circular building in the sanctuary of Athena Pronaia, and other architectural members with relief decoration.

Here visitors can admire four of the superb metopes of the tholos, which are excellently conceived and executed, with great boldness and sensitivity in the modelling of the figures. They are 7 cm. thick and measure 66 x 62.5 cm. The metopes were set above the 20 outer columns of the tholos and the architrave, and had relief scenes of an Amazonomachy and a Centauromachy. In the surviving metopes displayed on the restored section of the tholos in this room, are depicted:

a) A Centaur seizing a woman,

b) A rearing horse and a male figure,

c) An Amazon attacking a Greek who has fallen to his knees,

d) A man moving towards a votive column at which there stands a female figure.

This room also contains some very fragmentary metopes, some of them external, while some belong to the internal metopes that adorned the exterior circular wall of the cella.

These internal metopes are smaller, measuring 42 x 0.5 cm. and depict the labours of Theseus and Herakles.

Separate pedestals in the room support female figures dating from the early decades of the 4th c. BC, which probably came from the akroteria of various buildings.

Finally, visitors can see a Doric column capital from the exterior colonnade of the monuments, an internal Corinthian half-column that stood on the podium inside the cella, and a triglyph with its architrave block.

ROOM OF THE DAOCHOS MONUMENT

In this room visitors may see six of the nine statues from the 'family' dedication made by Daochos II, tetrach of Thessaly, in the sanctuary of Apollo.

The nine larger than life sized statues were placed on pedestals of local limestone. Eight of them, on inscribed pedestals, were portraits of Daochos, his forebears, and his son, while the ninth, which stood on an uninscribed base, probably depicted Apollo. An epigram on the base of the dedicator himself informs us that the monument was dedicated by Daochos to Apollo when he was hieromnemon of the Delphic Amphictyony between 336 and 332 BC.

The statues of this dedication were placed in chronological order from right to left. The statue of Apollo at the right is lost, and all that survives is the empty pedestal, with a wider socket than the others, indicating that the statue had a wider seating surface and was possibly heavier. To the left of this was Aknonios, a distant ancestor of Daochos, and his three sons: Agias, an Olympic victor in the pankration, Telemachos, whose statue is not preserved, and Agelaos, a runner. They were followed by of Agias's son, Daochos I (tetrarch of Thessaly), Daochos I's son Sisyphos I, and the latter's son Daochos II, who dedicated the group. All that survives of his statue are the shoes with crossed thongs. Finally, there was a statue of the dedicator's son, Sisyphos II.

The first statue on display is that of Agias, a famous pankratiast who won several victories in the Olympic, Nemean, Isthmian, and Pythian games. He is tall and depicted frontally, with the small head turned slightly to the side. He is the idealised type of athlete and has no individual characteristics. He was originally wearing a metal band, which is now lost. The facial expression, with its intense gaze and partly open mouth, conveys a sense of directness and energy.

The anatomical type of the sculpture renders not simply an outline figure, but a three-dimensional figure of imposing volume.

The figure of Agias recalls morphological aspirations similar to those of the school of Lysippos. A copy of the epigram of Agias found on the base of a bronze statue at Pharsala signed by Lysippos suggests that this statue may be a marble copy of Lysippos's bronze.

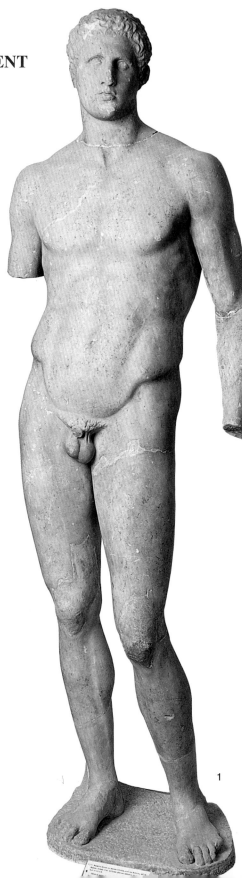

1

1. *The statue of Agias.*

2. *Statue of a philosopher.*

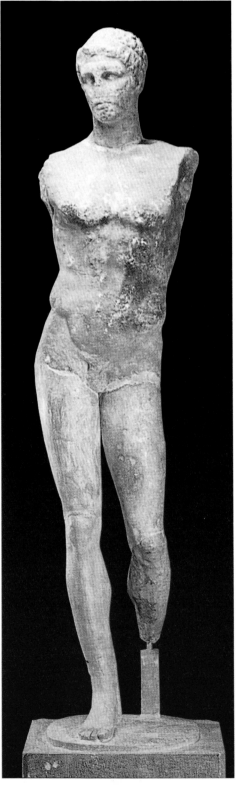

Some scholars go so far as to attribute the entire Daochos dedication to the school of the great sculptor, though this cannot be asserted with certainty.

The next statue on display is that of Sisyphos II, the son of Daochos II, the only static figure in the entire monument. It depicts a youth wearing a chlamys that is about to slip from his left shoulder. The entire weight of the figure is leaning against and supported on a hermaic stele of Archaic style which is carved of a piece with the torso. There are holes in the head for attaching a metal wreath. The stance of the youth suggests that the work is based on a model by Praxiteles.

The next statue is of the runner Agelaos, who is standing with his weight entirely supported on the right leg, with the left drawn backwards. Agelaos was a victor in the Pythian games, and has his arms raised to fasten the victory wreath in his hair. The tall proportions, naturalistic rendering, and idealised features of the work in general suggest that this is probably a later rendering of the Diadoumenos by Polykleitos.

There follows the statue of Sisyphos I (son of Daochos I), who is depicted as a warrior, wearing a short, girt chiton. A chlamys hangs from his left shoulder and his right arm is raised, possibly brandishing his sword or giving a command. Traces of paint are preserved on the figure, which is turned three-quarters to the viewer. The chiton hangs in thin, linear folds, rather than rich drapery. The overall stance was later used for statues of Roman emperors. Together with Agias, Sisyphos I is one of the most interesting statues of this group.

Aknonios, depicted in the following statue, is shown standing with his left leg relaxed and his left arm raised. He wears a short, girt chiton and a chlamys that was fastened by fibulae, as is clear from the holes in the right shoulder. The expansive gesture suggests that he was presenting his forebears to Apollo, who stood next to him.

The last statue displayed is that of Daochos I, son of Agias. He is standing with his right leg bent and wears a short chiton. He is completely covered by a heavy Macedonian chlamys and has his left arm folded across his breast.

3

All the dressed statues have attached limbs that were made of separate pieces of marble. They also wear shoes and socks that reach half way up the shins.

1. Statue of Sisyphos.
2. Statue of Agelaos.
3. Statue of Daochos.

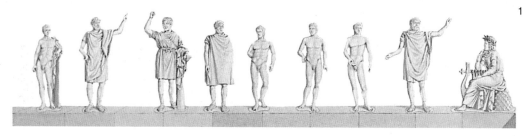

This room also contains one of the finest masterpieces in the Museum: the group of three young girls atop a stele crowned by acanthus leaves, from the sanctuary of Apollo. The total height of this dedication, which was made of pentelic marble, was 13 metres. The three young girls, who are apparently dancing, are each wearing a diaphanous peplos girt high beneath the breast and hanging down to the knees. Their left hands hang down holding the chitons, while the right hands are raised. The garments scarcely hide their soft flesh, allowing their well-formed bodies to show through. Their faces are lit by a faint smile and their legs seem to be executing a gentle dance step. On their heads they wear a polos which, together with the projecting acanthus leaves, supported a bronze tripod and cauldron. When this ensemble stood in the sanctuary it will have made an impressive effect with its great size and unusual design. The inscription on the base tells us it was dedicated by the Athenians between the years 335 and 325 BC. It probably depicts Pandrosos, Erse and Aglauros, the three daughters of Kekrops, the mythical king of Athens. The group is one of the finest expressions of Classical art.

Also in this room is a marble portrait of an old man, possibly a philosopher. The tranquil figure of the old man with his contemplative expression dates from 280-270 BC.

2

3

1. *Reconstruction of the monument of Daochos.*
2. *Headless statue of Sisyphos.*
3. *Statue of Alknonios.*
4. *Group of three dancing girls on a column.*

ROOM OF THE CHARIOTEER

The bronze charioteer displayed in this room is unquestionably the finest exhibit in the Delphi Museum. It was discovered during the French excavations of 1896 beneath the Sacred Way and is one of the most famous bronze objects created in the 5th c. BC. It should not be viewed as a self-contained statue but as part of a complex that also included a four-horse chariot on which the Charioteer stood, and a servant in front of it holding the reins. This restoration of the ensemble is dictated by other fragments of it that have been discovered, amongst them parts of three horse's legs, a bronze horse's tail, pieces of the chariot, a child's arm, and fragments of the reins.

The group depicted the moment when the Charioteer, rendered standing and life-size at 1.80 m., was receiving the applause of the crowd after his great victory in the race.

The ensemble was dedicated by Polyzalos of Gela, son of Deinomenes, of the family of Syracusan tyrants, after his victory in the chariot-race at the Pythian games in 478 BC or 474 BC. The tyrants of Syracuse were accustomed to make ostentatious displays of their wealth in their native land, through victories won in costly events such as the chariot-race and also through the dedications they erected at the major sanctuaries. Their victories at the pan-Hellenic games were also hymned by the great poets Pindar and Bacchylides.

On the base of the group was an inscription, part of which is preserved and which, when restored, tells us that 'I was dedicated by Polyzalos, victorious with his horses, son of Deinomenes, to whom he brought happiness, o glorious Apollo.' The first line is inscribed over an original inscription 'Polyzalos, ruler of Gela, dedicated the monument'. This was later erased, possibly because it referred explicitly to Polyzalos's rule at Gela, where his tyrannical regime was generally unpopular.

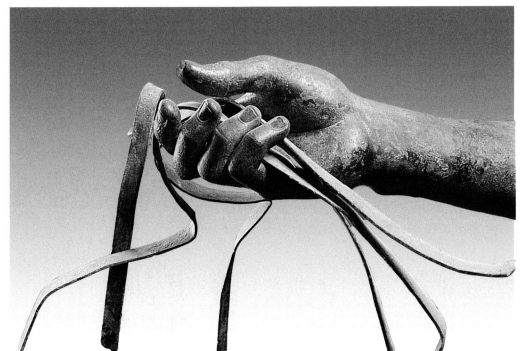

The Charioteer, a tall, athletic, broad-shouldered figure, wears the long, hieratic chiton usually worn by charioteers with straps around the shoulders preventing the garment from billowing in the wind. The chiton is girt high above the waist and the two straps passed under his arms and crossed high on his back, thus protecting the garment from blowing in the wind during the contest. The rich drapery on the chest stands in contrast to the column-like quality of the long skirt, the bottom of which, with the fine feet, would have been unseen. In his hands (only the right is now preserved) he held the reigns, and possibly also a whip. The body has a slight turn, avoiding a strictly frontal composition and giving the figure life. The posture is still rather Archaic in style but exudes a noble, elegant simplicity.

Reconstruction of the statue of the Charioteer (E. Krischen).

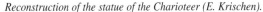

The slight turn of the body begins with the firmly placed feet and gradually rises up to the head, creating a proud figure and enlivening the work without disrupting the fluted folds of the long skirt. The body, which as we have seen is sculptured in the round at life size, is surmounted by an aristocratic head. The Charioteer's head, which is slightly turned towards the viewer, is still Archaic. The victory band, which had silver decoration, was fastened tight around the forehead and temples. The left half of the face is made wider than the other to correct an optical distortion. The tresses of hair are meticulously worked in low relief and frame the oval face, with its powerful jaw, slightly open mouth, fleshy lips, fairly full cheeks, and superb clear eyes, which have survived intact. The lips were made of a different alloy of bronze, and the large, almond-shaped eyes have inlaid enamel eyeballs and semiprecious stones for the irises. The work is a unique figure pulsating with life. The Charioteer's gaze, incomparable and attractive, seems to be fixed on something. No inner reflection, no passing or fleeting thought interrupts it, and there is no hesitation, however imperceptible or momentary. It is nonetheless a highly expressive, uniquely alive work, capturing the natural calm that follows upon the intensity and tension of the contest.

The exposed parts of the flesh are rendered with great care, capturing the pulse of life and tension in a super figure that was an idealised portrayal of the type of the great victor.

The sculptor is unknown. It was possibly by Pythagoras of Samos, who sought refuge in exile at Rhegium in Calabria. According to another view, it was the work of the great Athenian sculptor Kritias.

The surviving fragments of the bronze group are also exhibited in this room.

8140 Also on display in the room is a superb white kylix, with a depiction of Apollo seated on a diphros (a kind of stool, with no backrest), the crossed legs of which end in lion's paws. He wears a chiton, fastened at the shoulders by fibulae, and a purple himation. In an atmosphere of divine tranquillity he pours a libation of wine from the bowl in his right hand, while in his right he holds the lyre, his fingers resting on the strings.

The black bird depicted in front of him is probably a crow and may symbolise Koronis, the daughter of King Phlegyas, with whom Apollo fell in love and fathered Asklepios.

The kylix is contemporary with the Charioteer and dates from the decade 480-470 BC. The vase-painter is unknown.

White kylix depicting Apollo seated on a stool and holding his lyre.

ANTINOOS ROOM

Amongst the other exhibits in the final room, visitors will see the excellent statue of Antinoos, the favourite of the emperor Hadrian. The beautiful youth from Bithynia in Asia Minor was drowned in the flower of his youth in the waters of the Nile, having accompanied the Hadrian to Egypt in AD 130. Tradition has it that he gave his life to save Hadrian, who had a great regard for Classical Greece. Hadrian was passionately fond of the youth and after his death had him deified and erected statues of him in many cities and sanctuaries of the Greek world, and also founded a city called Antinoopolis in Egypt.

This statue, which depicts Antinoos as a god, was dedicated at Delphi by Aristotimos, the priest of Pythian Apollo. At Delphi, special honour was accorded to the companion of the emperor who showed such great interest in the city.

The work, carved from Parian marble and dedicated during the 130s AD, is one of the finest depictions of the famous youth and one of the final authentic creations of the Greek spirit of that period.

Antinoos is depicted naked, his head slightly inclined. The thick hair falls on to the forehead and at either side of the face, which is turned to the left, with its soft cheeks, rounded jaw, fleshy lips and dreaming eyes. The rich hair was restrained by a band, which was probably adorned with gold ivy leaves. The dark marble of the base intensifies the impression created by the gleaming white, polished body.

The feature that engages the attention of all who view the statue, however, is the melancholy, almost grieving gaze. The eyes are full of sorrow and appear to be bidding farewell to a period that was coming to an end, to be lost forever. This superb portrait is an excellent summation of the trends of a period that strove to resist its own inevitable decay and sought rebirth in a nostalgic resort to Classical models in both art and in religion. The beautiful, though melancholic youth embodies a temporary Classicism, and the noble figure is devoid of the liveliness exuded by Classical statues of naked youths, most of them athletes, which brim over with vigour and vitality.

Statue of Antinoos, with the Nymphs and Pan opposite (450 BC).

4070 Opposite the statue of Antinoos is displayed the headless hermaic stele of Plutarch AD 46-120), who was for many years priest of Apollo at Delphi. The inscription informs us that it was dedicated by the Chaironeians along with the people of Delphi.

4755 Next to it is a statue of a small boy holding a goose, dating from the end of the 3rd c. BC, and a male portrait head **1706** carved of Parian marble in the early 2nd c. BC. It probably depicts the Roman consul Titus Quintus Flamininus who defeated Philip V of Macedon at Kynoskephalai in 197 BC and proclaimed all the Greek cities free at the Isthmian games of the following year. A base was found during excavation that supported a bronze statue of Flamininus. In this head, in which he is portrayed as a young man, the excellent artist has worked the facial features with great care and consistency, and has gone beyond the bounds of a routine

sculpture to produce a complex picture of the consul's personality and individual character.

Next we see a charming statue of a young girl dating from the early 3rd c. BC, and a marble portrait from a hermaic stele depicting a male figure full of introspection, who was possibly a philosopher. It dates from the 2nd c. AD.

Visitors should also note the showcases in the last room. The first case is devoted mainly to vases of Early, Middle, and Late Helladic date, discovered during excavations at Krissa and its harbour, Kirrha. In the second case are displayed clay vases and figurines of the Late Helladic period (1400-1100 BC), from the cemeteries of Delphi, the sanctuary of Apollo, and the sanctuary of Athena Pronaia. The third case, finally, contains finds from the Korykeion Cave, a large cave on Mount Parnassos sacred to the god Pan and the Nymphs. The cave is near the acropolis of the prehistoric city at Lykoreia.

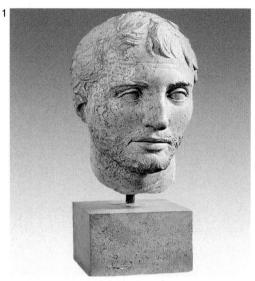

The items on display consist of humble dedications, most of them made of clay. We may note the terracotta plate depicting the contest between Apollo and Herakles for the Delphic tripod; also a black-figure plaque with a scene of Satyrs. The case also contains clay vases, terracotta and bronze figurines of female figures, animals, etc.

Outside the Museum is displayed a beautiful mosaic floor from the 5th c. AD Early Christian basilica discovered in the village of Delphi in 1959. It depicts floral motifs, animals and young people in very bright colours.

There is also a marble sarcophagus from the east cemetery of Delphi, on the lid of which is a depiction of the dead person reclining.

Finally, in the sheltered area in front of the Delphi Museum are housed architectural members from various buildings, a female statue, and many of the valuable inscriptions found at Delphi, which afford important evidence for the study of epigraphy.

1. Head of the Roman Titus Flamininus.
2. Bust of a man (3rd c. BC).
3. Statue of a young girl.
4. The statue of Antinoos.

INDEX

GLOSSARY

Adyton: the most sacred room of an ancient Greek temple, entered only by priests and initiates.

Akroterion: decorative architectural member placed at the apex and two ends of a pediment.

Alabastron: small vase used mainly for perfumes.

Aryballos: small globular vase to contain oil.

Cavea: the auditorium of an ancient theatre. Semicircle usually formed in the side of a hill, often completed with the aid of man-made deposits.

(Dekati) Tithe: A system of taxation equivalent to one tenth of annual argicultural produce or income.

Distyle in antis: temple with the two side walls projecting beyond the facade, with two columns between them.

Echinos: convex moulding below the abacus, usually of a Doric capital.

(Erisinoto) Back: That part of a seat or chair on which the back of the seated person rests.

Frieze: decorative zone above the architrave in the entablature of an ancient temple. In the Doric order, it was decorated with metopes and triglyphs, while in the Ionic order it had a continuous relief.

Impost block: block in the shape of an inverted, truncated pyramid placed between the abacus and the capital of a column.

Krater: vase used for mixing wine with water.

Kylix: cup with horizontal handles.

Lekythos: container for aromatic oil. Funerary lekythoi were common in the ancient world.

Metope: stone slab either plain or carved in relief; alternated with the triglyphs in the Doric order.

Peripteral: temple with an exterior colonnade on all sides.

Phiale: two-handled bowl, normally used for libations.

Pit: used in the ancient world for earlier, destroyed dedications and sculptures; also to protect cult objects from being profaned.

Prostyle: temple with a row of columns in front of the cella.

Strigil: long bronze or iron scraper used by athletes to clean the oil and dust from their bodies after training.

Stylobate: the upper part of the base of a temple, on which the columns rested directly.

Terrace: level area higher than the surrounding terrain, either natural or man-made.

Treasury: small building in the form of a temple, normally dedicated by a city in a large sanctuary as an indication of its gratitude. It served as a repository for precious dedications.

Triglyph: decorative element in a Doric temple, consisting of grooves; alternated with the metopes.

BIBLIOGRAPHY

Pausanias, *Description of Greece*, X, 5, 5-32, I (*Phokika*).
History of the Greek Nation, Ekdotike Athenon.

Manolis Andronikos, *Delphi*, Ekdotike Athenon, Athens 1988.
D. Goudis, Το Μαντείον των Δελφών, 1935.
Chr. Karouzos, Δελφοί, 1974.
Vasilios Ch. Petrakos, Δελφοί, Klio Editions, Athens 1977.
Marilena Carabatea, *Archaeological Guide to Delphi*, Adam Editions.
Photis Petsas, Δελφοί, Krini Editions, Athens 1983.

P. Amandry, *La mantige apollinienne à Delphes*, 1950.
H.R. Dodds, *The Greeks and the Irrational*.
M. Delacourt, *L'oracle de Delphes*, 1955.
R. Flacelière, *Greek Oracles*.
H.W. Parke, *Greek Oracles*.
H.W. Parke and D.E.N. Normell, *The Delphic Oracle*, 1956.
G. Roux, *Delphi*.

Text: ANNA MARANDI
Text edited by: DAFNI CHRISTOU
Design: MICHALIS LATSENERE - EVI DAMIRI

Colour separations - printing: M. TOUBIS S.A.